Trauma-Informed Theology

Trauma-Informed Theology

An African American Intimate Partner Violence Intervention Tool for the Pentecostal Clergy

BRIDGET P. ROBINSON

Foreword by Archbishop Alfred A. Owens Jr.

WIPF & STOCK · Eugene, Oregon

TRAUMA-INFORMED THEOLOGY
An African American Intimate Partner Violence Intervention Tool for the Pentecostal Clergy

Copyright © 2025 Bridget P. Robinson. All rights reserved. Except for brief quotations in critical publications or reviews, no part of this book may be reproduced in any manner without prior written permission from the publisher. Write: Permissions, Wipf and Stock Publishers, 199 W. 8th Ave., Suite 3, Eugene, OR 97401.

Wipf & Stock
An Imprint of Wipf and Stock Publishers
199 W. 8th Ave., Suite 3
Eugene, OR 97401

www.wipfandstock.com

PAPERBACK ISBN: 979-8-3852-3611-4
HARDCOVER ISBN: 979-8-3852-3612-1
EBOOK ISBN: 979-8-3852-3613-8

This body of work is dedicated to women victim-survivors of intimate partner violence sitting in the pews. No More Holy Hush!

The Spirit of the Lord is upon me because he hath anointed me to preach the gospel to the poor; he hath sent me to heal the brokenhearted, to preach deliverance to the captives, and recovering of sight to the blind, to set at liberty them that are bruised.

—Luke 4:18

To appoint unto them that mourn in Zion, to give unto them beauty for ashes, the oil of joy for mourning, the garment of praise for the spirit of heaviness; that they might be called trees of righteousness, the planting of the Lord, that he might be glorified.

—Isa 61:3

Contents

List of Illustrations ix

Foreword xi

Preface xiii

Acknowledgements xvii

Introduction xxi

Realize 1

Recognize 26

Respond 44

Resist Retraumatization 62

Module One: Realize 77

Module Two: Recognize 95

Module Three: Respond 113

Module Four: Resist Retraumitization 139

Closing Word 161

About the Author 163

Bibliography 165

List of Illustrations

Figure 1. Power and Control | 3
Figure 2. Cycles of Violence | 3
Figure 3. Intersectionality | 17
Figure 4. The Umbrella of Protection | 22
Figure 5. Christianity in Africa | 27
Figure 6. World Christian Population by Region, 2010 and 2050 | 28
Figure 7. Rate of Women Killed by Partner or Family Members per 100,000 Population | 29
Figure 8. Christians by Movement | 30
Figure 9. Pentecostals and Charismatics by Region | 30
Figure 10. Patriarchy | 32
Figure 11. A Hermeneutic Phenomenology of African American Women's Lived Experiences with IPV in Pentecostal Ministry | 37
Figure 12. God's Umbrella of Protection (Complementary) | 42
Figure 13. The Four Fs of Trauma Response: Fight, Flight, Freeze, Fawn | 48
Figure 14. A Trauma-Informed Approach (Four Rs) | 50
Figure 15. Knowles's 5 Assumptions of Adult Learners | 66
Figure 16. Knowles's 4 Principles of Andragogy | 66
Figure 17. "Gye Nyame" African Adinkra Symbol | 69
Figure 18. "Nsoromma," African Adinkra Symbol | 70
Figure 19. "Matie Masie," African Adinkra Symbol | 70
Figure 20. "Akoma Ntoso," African Adinkra Symbol | 71
Figure 21. "Denkyem," African Adinkra Symbol | 71
Figure 22. "Sankofa," African Adinkra Symbol | 72
Figure 23. Dick and Carey Model for Instructional Design | 73
Figure 24. ADDIE Training and Curriculum Development | 74
Figure 25. Power and Control Wheel | 84

List of Illustrations

Figure 26. Christian Power and Control Wheel | 85
Figure 27. Cycle of Abuse | 88
Figure 28. Intersectionality of IPV for African American Women | 103
Figure 29. Patriarchy | 104
Figure 30. Intersectionality of Pentecostal Risk Factors for IPV | 106
Figure 31. "Gye Nyamme" African Adinkra Symbol | 132
Figure 32. "Nsoromma," African Adinkra Symbol | 132
Figure 33. "Matie Masie," African Adinkra Symbol | 133
Figure 34. "Akoma Ntoso," African Adinkra Symbol | 133
Figure 35. "Denkyem," African Adinkra Symbol | 134
Figure 36. "Sankofa," African Adinkra Symbol | 134

Foreword

Archbishop Alfred A. Owens Jr.

As I reflect on Dr. Bridget P. Robinson's life and work, I am reminded of God's miraculous power to heal and restore. For 25 years, I have had the privilege of being her pastor, watching her overcome trauma and intimate partner violence (IPV) to experience profound spiritual, mental, and physical growth. Dr. Robinson is a woman of faith, a powerful prayer warrior, and a gifted teacher, ready and able to serve in ministry.

As her spiritual father, I have seen Dr. Robinson's deep faith, commitment to prayer, and calling to ministry firsthand. She is not only a gifted educator in both Christian and secular settings, but she is also a passionate advocate for the most vulnerable in society. Her service on the Ministerial Alliance Board at Greater Mount Calvary Holy Church and in numerous other ministries reflects her heart for women and children, especially those affected by IPV.

In *Trauma-Informed Theology: An African American Intimate Partner Violence Intervention Tool for the Pentecostal Clergy*, Dr. Robinson combines her personal experiences with her extensive academic and pastoral knowledge. This book is more than just a curriculum; it is a crucial resource that empowers clergy to effectively address IPV in the African American community. Dr. Robinson also addresses the deep-seated trauma rooted in the legacy of slavery and the Jim Crow era, challenging the Church to confront how these histories shape our theology and our responses to suffering.

This work offers practical, trauma-informed care principles that will equip ministers and laypeople alike to foster healing, spiritual growth, and a restorative theology for women impacted by IPV. Dr. Robinson's life and her work embody the very message she shares—God's love and healing can transform even the most broken situations.

FOREWORD

I wholeheartedly recommend this book. It is a powerful call to action for the Church to engage with the realities of IPV and offer true healing.

Get ready to be changed and moved to action.

Archbishop Alfred A. Owens Jr.
Founding Pastor
Greater Mount Calvary Holy Church
Washington, DC

Preface

Given the current situation in our country, where presidential executive orders will silence and make invisible victims/survivors of intimate partner violence (IPV), especially African American women, it is clearer why God has commissioned me to be a mouthpiece to advocate for IPV awareness. While working on this manuscript, I quickly realized that, in the short amount of time since I completed my dissertation, officials had updated both government and non-government websites to reflect President Trump's executive orders. These orders mandate the removal of diversity, equity, inclusion, and accessibility (DEIA) from readily available sources, which significantly impacts data availability and could skew our understanding of social issues.

Because of this executive order, websites have chosen not to report IPV statistics by ethnic groups or race, instead reporting only general statistics about males and females. Taking a blanket approach across ethnic groups and race to mitigate the problem of IPV can cause harm, as it fails to consider the intersectionality of individuals' identities and the culture and complexity of their communities. This framework of "colorblindness" in a society shaped by Eurocentric ideology renders other cultures invisible, which influences our politics, economics, and social structures, fostering the erroneous concept of one size fits all.

As clergy, our role as shepherds of God's people is to understand and address the unique struggles and stories of every flock member. The current Trump administration's DEIA executive orders, while aiming for unity and fairness, adopts a colorblind approach that overlooks the sacred particularities of God's diverse creation. When policies disregard cultural identity and context, they risk further silencing voices that have long been unheard—especially the voices of Black women.

My work takes a different path, one rooted in empathy, truth-telling, and the Gospel's call to justice. I provide culturally competent IPV data tailored to African American women not as a critique, but as an act of care, because faithful ministry begins with truly seeing. This effort is part of a broader pastoral commitment to respond not only to pain but to the systems that perpetuate it. Let us continue to build a Church that listens, learns, and loves well together.

One in four women will experience IPV in their lifetime. Black women, who account for 14 percent of the U.S. population, are disproportionately affected, with nearly 45 percent of them having experienced some form of IPV or domestic violence.[1] A data analysis suggests that Black women are three times more likely than White women to be murdered by an intimate partner, and Black women represent 31 percent of domestic violence mortalities.[2] This underscores the urgent need for action to address the disproportionate impact of IPV on Black women.

At the crossroads where our different identities meet, the idea that "one size fits all" falls apart. To truly understand trauma-informed theology, that sacred place where our deepest wounds and God's healing grace come together, we must make space for many voices and stories. I come to this sacred work as a heterosexual African American woman living with low vision, shaped by the rich spiritual traditions of my Pentecostal and Holiness upbringing in South Carolina. This is the lens God has given me, and through it, I offer what I've learned with care, humility, and hope.

Growing up in the church, I always wondered why women were limited in upward mobility and leadership. Why women could not grace the sacred pulpit and why they could not preach the Gospel of Jesus Christ. These questions were not just academic for me; they were deeply personal. I often questioned the restrictions on women not wearing makeup, jewelry, slacks, or the color red. Women were seen but not heard in this context; patriarchal social structures silenced them to a certain extent. Unbeknownst to me at the time, my theology lay within a microcosmos known as the Black church.

One Sunday evening during church, we welcomed a guest preacher from the continent of Africa. After the service, he gave me a gentle smile and asked, "What do you want to be when you grow up?"

---

1. Bent-Goodley, Zonicle, and Romero-Chandler, "Perceptions, Help-Seeking, and High-Risk Domestic Violence in Black Communities," 9536–62.

2. Bent-Goodley, Zonicle, and Romero-Chandler, "Perceptions, Help-Seeking, and High-Risk Domestic Violence in Black Communities," 9536–62.

Without missing a beat, I said, "I want to be a missionary in Africa."

Even as a young girl, I was moved by the images I had seen on television of women and children facing famine, disease, and deep need. Those scenes didn't just tug at my heart; they ignited a call. This call to serve, to stand with the most vulnerable among us, is one I carry with me every day.

That early calling never left me. It grew deeper with time, shaped by life, prayer, and purpose. In my very DNA, I carry the legacy of the African continent and the resilience of ancestors who endured the brutal legacy of colonialism with unwavering faith. This ancestral connection has been a guiding force in my mission to serve and advocate for the most vulnerable.

My journey, rooted in a Pentecostal tradition, has always been about healing and advocacy. It's about listening to the Spirit, seeking justice, and believing in the transforming power of God to restore what's been broken. My faith has been the guiding light in this journey, and I hope it can also be a source of strength and inspiration for you.

My journey is a testament to the power of faith and resilience. Despite early childhood trauma and sexual abuse within my church community and the daunting diagnosis of sarcoidosis and two incurable eye diseases (uveitis and glaucoma), I held onto my faith. I survived a marriage marred by IPV, and, with my two small children, I fled for our lives on a Greyhound bus to Washington, DC. I found my voice and accepted my call to the ministry and higher education.

Today, I hold a Doctor of Ministry in Spirit-filled Global Leadership in the African Diaspora from George Fox University, a program in partnership with Jakes Divinity School. My research focused on trauma-informed theology and IPV within the African American community. I also hold a Master of Arts in Community Health Promotion and Education from Trinity Washington University and a bachelor's degree in psychology from the University of the District of Columbia. My divine assignment is to serve women and children at the crossroads of life, breaking the chains of trauma and abuse. I am a licensed evangelist under The Mount Calvary Holy Church of America, Inc., and an active Greater Mount Calvary Holy Church member, serving on the Ministerial Alliance Board. I am also an accomplished writer, health communicator, educator, and author of *My Eyes Dare to Believe* and *A Single Woman's Guide to Protecting and Defending Her Celibacy in God*.

My professional background includes extensive community outreach and partnership-building experience with material and curriculum development, grant writing, secondary education, and Christian education. I have experience working with families with histories of trauma, domestic violence, mental health, substance abuse, and incarceration, as well as those at risk for child abuse. I am an emergent leader in the field of trauma-informed theology and an IPV advocate, advocating for social justice for all forms of gender-based violence.

My experiences and academic background have given me the credentialing and expertise to create and develop this curriculum. I am confident in my ability to bring hope, healing, and deliverances to humanity through the wonder-working power of the Holy Spirit.

Acknowledgements

I BEGIN WITH HEARTFELT gratitude and praise to God for his perfect love, guidance, strength, and perfecting presence throughout this journey. Thank You, God, for empowering me with the anointing of the scribe and for helping me and strengthening me in completing this work. God, you told me many years ago that I am parchment, animal skins prepared for writing your truths in the earth realm so that Your will be done on earth as it is in heaven. Your guidance and inspiration were instrumental in every word I wrote. Thank You for trusting me to write this sacred work and to be a living epistle in this world of time.

Thank you, Archbishop Alfred A. Owens Jr. and co-pastor Susie C. Owens (Emeritus). Thank you for providing "bread" in Washington, DC, for 58 years at Greater Mount Calvary Holy Church. You are loving shepherds; you feed the sheep, protect the sheep, and ensure the sanctuary is a safe place to receive prayer, salvation, healing, and deliverance. Thank you both for being my spiritual parents. You nurtured me back to health, emotionally and spiritually, at a critical time when trauma shook my theology. This work was a healing and post-traumatic growth process, and your leadership and encouragement to pursue higher education in a Pentecostal setting are greatly appreciated. I am thankful to be a part of your ministry legacy. I love you.

Thank you, Mrs. Ethel "Honey" Belcher, for 12 unforgettable years of guidance and grace. Your wisdom in Christian education shaped me not just as a teacher but as a vessel for healing, especially for those carrying unseen wounds. You taught me to see beauty every day in every learner. "Beautiful, beautiful, beautiful," you'd always say, and now I understand. Teaching is sacred work, a part of the fivefold ministry. Your legacy lives on in me and in every life I touch. You will always hold a special place in my heart. I want to express my sincerest gratitude to you. Love you.

Acknowledgements

Dr. Stuart A. Cocanougher, thank you for your invaluable guidance, constant support, and prayer throughout my research. Your wisdom and encouragement have been crucial in helping me complete my research for this book. I am deeply grateful to Jakes Divinity School and George Fox University, Portland Seminary, for their partnership and signature Doctor of Ministry program, Spirit-filled Global Leadership in the African Diaspora. This program, which focuses on equipping leaders for effective ministry in the African Diaspora, has been a vital part of my journey, preparing me for the unique challenges and opportunities in this context. Special thanks to Drs. Valerie Crumpton, Solomon Waigwa, Cynthia James, Clifford Berger, Darcy Hansen, and Loren Kerns; their dedication to fostering spiritual and academic growth has been invaluable. I am thankful for cohort two of the program, whose mutual support in ministry is priceless.

I cannot express enough gratitude to God for blessing me with the opportunity to encounter a guardian angel, Jen Macnab. Your kindness is truly infectious, and I am sincerely thankful for the transformational God-moment conversations we shared. Your resourcefulness has been a constant source of support as I navigated through my doctoral program. You are light.

I am thankful for the generous financial support from Diakonos Solutions, Portland Seminary, and Jakes Divinity School. Their support has allowed me to focus on my research and writing, and I am deeply grateful for their commitment to fostering academic and spiritual growth.

Rochelle Deans, my editor, deserves my sincere appreciation. Your professionalism, attention to detail, and unwavering commitment to excellence have been invaluable throughout the writing process. Beyond your editorial expertise, your thoughtful coaching and encouragement have helped me grow as a writer, and your friendship has made this journey all the more meaningful. I am deeply thankful for the time, care, and insight you've shared with me, and I will always be grateful for your support. Thank you for helping bring this work to fruition gracefully and precisely.

Whit Robinson, my gifted graphic designer, what can I say? You always come through when it matters most. Thank you for your professionalism, sharp eye, and thoughtful feedback. Your creativity and support have been invaluable.

I also wish to express my gratitude to the study participants, whose significant contributions have been invaluable in shaping the research and its profound impact on future generations and the church.

Acknowledgements

To my beloved children, Jeffery Alexander Fleming Jr. and Hadassah Vashti Fleming, and my precious grandchildren, Nehemiah, Mila, and Jeremiah: Words cannot fully express my gratitude for your love, support, and understanding throughout this journey. Your patience and encouragement have been a constant source of strength to me. You have been my hope, inspiration, and joy; your prayers lifted me when I needed it most. Reflecting on this milestone, I am reminded of the legacy we are building together in ministry and education. This journey is a personal achievement and a testament to the values of faith, resilience, and a commitment to lifelong learning that we pass down through generations. I pray that you carry forward this legacy, embracing the power of knowledge, purpose, and service to others.

Introduction

AT ONE POINT, I believed that I had "abuse" written on my forehead because of my traumatic experiences in childhood and surviving an abusive marriage. I know that trauma can change the way you see God. In my early twenties, I was angry with God because of the abuse I endured. My spiritual belief system was compromised. I did not go to church for six years after I fled from the grips of my abusive husband in South Carolina to Washington, DC, in 1993. After wandering in the wilderness, I joined Greater Mount Calvary Holy Church. The first thing my pastor, Archbishop Alfred A. Owens Jr., did was refer me to Christian counseling, a service my church provides at no cost. I grew spiritually and mentally because my church practiced the principles of trauma-informed theology, even though that term had not yet been coined. Because of this life-transformational experience, I am assured God had called me to the vocation to work with women and children impacted by trauma. I also pray for the continual transformation of my mind, body, and spirit as God's vessel to be the mouthpiece for women and children at the crossroads of life.

Trauma-Informed Theology: An African American Intimate Partner Violence Intervention Tool for the Pentecostal Clergy expands the body of knowledge of IPV, trauma, and trauma-informed theology. The real-life ministry voices captured in this body of work magnify the opportunity the church has to respond to the needs of African American women who have experienced IPV in their lifetime. The social and cultural context of the African American experience during colonization and post-colonization leads to African American women experiencing higher rates of IPV, so the primary objective of this intervention tool is to increase the awareness of IPV among Pentecostal clergy.

The Black church has consistently served as a steadfast source of hope for the community. However, church leaders may not be aware of the profound effects of IPV many African American women experience, despite the concerning rate at which IPV occurs. This intervention tool carefully examines the risk factors present in Pentecostal ministry that may impede clergy members from fully comprehending, recognizing, and responding to this trauma, and thus potentially retraumatizing women who have experienced IPV.

Trauma-informed theology provides the framework for this curriculum. The progression of the "4Rs" of trauma-informed care, in chronological order (realize, recognize, respond, and resist retraumatization), is the foundation for this curriculum's instructional design.

Chapter 1—Realize emphasizes the need for clergy members to understand IPV and the unique factors contributing to its heightened prevalence among African Americans. It's crucial to consider historical trauma, systemic racism, and patriarchal structure through the context of Pentecostalism. Your role in this understanding is vital.

Chapter 2—Recognize highlights the importance of clergy members recognizing the potential risk factors within the culture of Pentecostal theology that hinder their ability to effectively understand, acknowledge, address, and avoid retraumatizing victims of IPV in a ministry setting. This knowledge empowers you and instills confidence in your ability to be prepared and proactive.

Chapter 3—Respond calls for the integration of trauma-informed theology to deepen our understanding of IPV. This section offers a foundational framework that weaves together trauma-informed principles and biblical truths—serving as an anchor for applying these insights within the Pentecostal ministry context. It invites clergy to respond with spiritual conviction and informed compassion.

Chapter 4—Resist Retraumatization outlines the theoretical framework for developing the IPV curriculum, including adult learning theories, cultural competency, and the practical implementation of the curriculum. It equips you with tools and strategies to handle IPV confidently and effectively in your ministry.

The curriculum is designed to help clergy comprehensively understand IPV and its impact specifically on African American women in the Pentecostal community. It is an intervention tool to mitigate passivity among the clergy, empowering them to consider their social and cultural context and advocate for the victim-survivors sitting in their pews. This empowerment is a significant step forward in addressing IPV within the church. The intervention tool opens a dialogue about trauma by raising awareness, improving knowledge and attitudes, providing interactive activities and advocacy, and making recommendations for trauma-informed ministries by giving people language to talk about trauma and IPV, creating a safe environment, and addressing cultural, historical, and gender issues.

The curriculum trains clergy to react effectively to trauma within their communities in and outside the church, ensuring pastoral care is supported by theological precepts and the principles of trauma-informed care. Trauma-informed Pentecostal theology has the capacity to combine liberating and empowering elements of faith, which deepens gender sensitivity to the lived realities of abuse survivors. It is through the power of the Holy Spirit—the very breath of God—that true transformation takes place. That same Spirit works in the lives of both the minister and the survivor, leading them on a journey of spiritual healing, emotional renewal, and restored relationships. As Pentecostal clergy, we are not just seen but deeply trusted as spiritual guides, and it is our sacred responsibility to walk alongside those who are hurting, pointing them to the healing power of God.

Applying trauma-informed theology in a sacred setting fosters safety, trustworthiness, peer support, collaboration, empowerment, and cultural consideration of its parishioners—the guiding principles of trauma-informed care. Thus, it empowers clergy to reimage God's love and mercy because they will gain knowledge and confidence to be effective agents of transformation, advocating for those experiencing IPV by breaking the chains of abuse and silence in communities of violence and oppression. This intersectionality approach is vital as it provides perspective to not only the personal trauma of abuse but also the communal and transgenerational wounds of African Americans that have been exacerbated by systemic racism and social injustice, especially toward Black women.

This training manual is primarily for the Pentecostal clergy. The term "clergy" is a designation within the ecclesiastical realm that refers to women and men who have received ordination as religious leaders within the Christian church. The secondary audience is pastors, ministers, church leaders, laity, and those within the sphere of influence in the African American community who are committed to making the church a safe, supportive place for all individuals, particularly African American women who have experienced IPV. This work is also intended for an academic audience, as it provides new contributions to the body of scholarship in trauma-informed theology, hermeneutics, homiletics, biblical interpretation, gender-based violence, feminist theology, womanist theology, and gender-sensitivity ministry.

Introduction

We now turn to Chapter One, where we lay the foundation for this work by grounding it in both lived experience and theological reflection. This section centers on the urgency of understanding IPV within the African American community and the vital role Pentecostal clergy play in responding faithfully. To "realize" is our first step in recognizing the weight of historical trauma, systemic racism, and patriarchal structures that shape the lived reality of IPV.

Clergy, your awareness, and your response are not optional; they are essential for healing, justice, and the kind of Spirit-led ministry that reflects God's heart.

1

Realize

Introduction

THEOLOGY MATTERS IN OUR everyday lives, often in ways we don't even realize. We all engage in "ordinary theology," a way of thinking and talking about God that shapes how we see the world and interact with others. This kind of theology isn't based on formal academic education; it's the natural expression of beliefs that we form just by living and experiencing life as believers.[1]

Our theology, whether ordinary or academic, is not formed in a vacuum. It's shaped by the culture we live in. We all start out in life with a blank slate, without preconceived ideas about God. Our understanding of God develops as we grow and learn from our culture and experiences. Jeff Astley explains that our theology comes together through what we see, hear, and experience in the world around us.[2] Our culture shapes it, whether through the theology we learn from church, our families, or just observing others.

For those in ministry, understanding and utilizing ordinary theology is not just beneficial, but essential. By listening and observing how everyday believers think and talk about their faith, pastors and church leaders can better engage with people about their faith, from teaching and apologetics to evangelism and pastoral care.[3] Ordinary theology isn't just something to talk about—it's something to listen to and learn from because it's often the starting point for deeper theological understanding.

---

1. Astley, *Ordinary Theology*, 56.
2. Astley, *Ordinary Theology*, 57–82.
3. Astley, *Ordinary Theology*, 147.

Understanding "ordinary theology," then, is not just a theoretical exercise, but a practical necessity. It is the foundation of academic theology and the key to addressing the real issues that congregations face. Pastors and church leaders, armed with this understanding, can find real-world, practical solutions. By understanding their community's everyday theology, they can create better ways to teach, guide, and support their people in their spiritual journeys.

A Story

An African American young lady who attended a church in the city experienced early childhood trauma. She was active in children's ministry and the junior missionary board. She met her husband in the church and the pastor officiated the marriage ceremony. She suffered physical, emotional, and spiritual abuse within the marriage. The church doctrine held a stance against divorce. She petitioned the pastor for marriage counseling; he corrected the husband with words of wisdom and prayed for them. She approached the pastor again without her husband and shared that her husband continued to beat her. The pastor recommended she "go home and pray." No resources were made available to her, nor were any interventions. The abused woman continued to attend church; she was seen sitting in the pews, but she had no voice, silenced with a holy hush. Despair and disillusionment enveloped her mind, a broken vessel—a life of trauma at home and even at the hands of the church, where God dwells.

The Problem

One in four women experience intimate partner violence (IPV).[4] Ministry leaders may not understand the impact of these experiences on women. The CDC defines "IPV as abuse or aggression in a romantic relationship of present or past spouses or dating partners," including physical violence, sexual violence, stalking, and psychological aggression.[5] I will use IPV and domestic violence (DV) interchangeably throughout this research.

Understanding the meaning of IPV helps to conceptualize the pervasiveness of the crime.

---

4. Centers for Disease Control and Prevention, "Fast Facts: Preventing Intimate Partner Violence."

5. Centers for Disease Control and Prevention, "Fast Facts."

REALIZE

Figure 1. Power and Control[6]

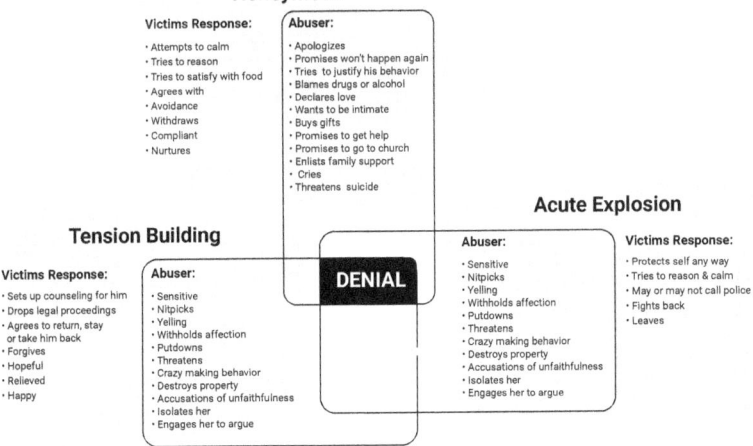

Figure 2. Cycles of Violence[7]

(Adapted from Lenore Walker, *The Battered Woman*, 1979)

6. The Duluth Model, theduluthmodel.org.
7. Adapted from Walker, *The Battered Woman*.

Far too often, church leaders remain unaware of the deep and lasting impact of IPV has on the lives of many, especially African American women, within our congregations. As shepherds of God's people, we must understand the weight of this crisis. The following statistics reflect the reality of those who sit in our pews, often suffering in silence.

- One in four women and one in ten men in the U.S. have reported experiencing IPV.[8]
- 35 percent of female IPV survivors and over 11 percent of male survivors experience physical injury.[9]
- One in five homicides in the U.S. is committed by a current or former intimate partner.[10]
- IPV prevalence by race among women:[11]
  » 45 percent of Black women
  » 37.3 percent of white women
  » 34.4 percent of Hispanic women
  » 18.3 percent of Asian women
- Among African Americans:[12]
  » 41.2 percent of Black women and 36.3 percent of Black men have experienced physical IPV in their lifetime.
  » 38 percent of Black women and 24.4 percent of Black men have experienced sexual IPV in their lifetime.

There may be unique risk factors for IPV in the African American community, considering the social and cultural context of the African American experience of 400 years of slavery, ninety years of Jim Crow, sixty years of "separate but equal," and thirty-five years of state-sanctioned redlining[13] to present-day "Neo Crow."[14]

---

8. Centers for Disease Control and Prevention, "Fast Facts."
9. Centers for Disease Control and Prevention, "Fast Facts."
10. Centers for Disease Control and Prevention, "Fast Facts."
11. Smith, et al., "The National Intimate Partner and Sexual Violence Survey," 117–18.
12. Breiding, "Prevalence and Characteristics," E11–12.
13. Coates, "The Case For Reparations."
14. Menakem, *My Grandmother's Hands*, 74.

African American Community

The African American community has its roots forever connected to the cruel and violent institution of slavery in America. This historical trauma in the African American community is believed to have passed from generation to generation.[15] This legacy of transferred abuse in the African American community can be traced back to ancestors who may have internalized the enslavers' abuse model from their slave plantations. It is conceivable that the seeds bearing from the institution of slavery have obstructed social, political, and micro-systems, contributing to the higher incidence rates of IPV in African Americans.[16] One theory to explain IPV risk factors is Post-Traumatic Slave Syndrome (PTSS), a theory developed by Joy DeGruy Leary. PTSS explains the origin of numerous adaptive survival behaviors observed in African American communities across the US and the African diaspora, stemming from the historical experience of child slavery.[17] She argues that African Americans sustain traumatic psychological and emotional injury from institutionalized racism, social injustices, and inequalities that continue to oppress descendants of enslaved Africans.[18]

Another framework to consider in explaining the higher prevalence of IPV in the African American community is Feminist Political Theory. A Feminist Political Theory provides a viewpoint on the African American men's struggle to obtain masculinity in a patriarchal society dominated by white males that leave limited upward mobility for him and his internal conflict with the African American "matriarch" community.[19] In the social context of this duality, the African American male may take on a hypermasculine personification to achieve social status and identity and neglect his masculine role as a protector.[20] Hypermasculinization in Black males may be rooted in slavery; therefore, understanding the social and cultural context and the impact of slavery on the African American community requires applying the "psychoanalytic concepts of projection, splitting, and projective identification" to diagnose the problem's root causes and develop

---

15. American Psychological Association Dictionary, "Intergenerational Trauma."
16. Taft, et al., "Intimate Partner Violence," 50–58.
17. DeGruy, *Post-Traumatic Slave Syndrome*, 59, 105.
18. DeGruy, *Post-Traumatic Slave Syndrome*, 59, 105.
19. Brice-Baker, "Domestic Violence," 23–38.
20. Majors and Billson, *Cool Pose*, quoted in Taft, et al., "Intimate Partner Violence," 50–58.

culturally specific IPV intervention tools.[21] This hypermasculine personification, then, is another potential risk for IPV in the African American community.

African American Women

A quote by Edwidge Danticat, "We are ugly, but we are here," grabs our attention.[22] This quote is not about the aesthetics of beauty; instead, the word "ugly" denotes the groups of women of the African diaspora that are overlooked and pushed to the margins of society.

Bell and Mathis point out that the American culture has scraped away the feminine characteristics from African American women since slavery, assigning them masculine attributes; femininity is ascribed as the birthright of white women.[23] They suggest that America cultivated the perception that femininity and fragility are related to women's safety and regard, both of which are associated with white women. In contrast, non-femininity includes independent, uncontrollable, overpowering attributes associated with African American women.[24] The view that African American women are "Black Superwomen" is unrealistic in American culture.[25] However, African American women may nevertheless internalize the concept, resulting in low reporting of IPV incidents. The underreporting may explain the lack of responsiveness of society (i.e., culturally appropriate interventions and research) regarding the plight of these women in crisis. This perception of African American women perpetuates the viewpoint of blaming the victim, suggesting that she provoked her relationship partner.

During the focus groups and interviews I conducted, the "Black Superwoman" syndrome surfaced as a topic: " . . . we are taught that we are strong. We are taught that we are resilient."[26] However, having a superhero label attached to African American women could increase their vulnerability to IPV.

These unfavorable images also influence African American men's attitudes and perceptions about African American women, impeding their

---

21. Al'uqdah, Maxwell, and Hill, "Intimate Partner Violence," 877–84.
22. Danticat, "We Are Ugly, But We Are Here."
23. Bell and Mattis, "The Importance of Cultural Competence," 515–32.
24. Bell and Mattis, "The Importance of Cultural Competence."
25. Bell and Mattis, "The Importance of Cultural Competence."
26. Study Participant 3.

interpersonal relationships and increasing the risk of IPV. Tameka L. Gillum conducted a community-based study in 2002 with a sample of 221 African American males in Detroit, Michigan. The study incorporated a two-pronged approach: first, to examine African American men's views about African American women; second, to determine whether acceptance of violence against African American women relates to the stereotypical images.[27] The two images investigated were "Jezebel" and "Matriarch." The Jezebel stereotype portrays a woman who is excessively assertive, is driven by sexual desires, and engages in promiscuous behavior.[28] The matriarch is described as not having feminine features and has the power to emasculate African American men.[29] The study assessment tool was the *Perceptions of African American Women Scale*, a twenty-seven-item measure designed to explore if African American men hold stereotypical views of African women, including three subscales: Matriarch, Jezebel, and positive perceptions.[30] The belief is that the Matriarch and Jezebel stereotypical images can convince African men that African American women can emasculate them and that they need to have their sexual appetite controlled. The images suggest that men must dominate in intimate partner relationships to obtain power and control over women.[31] Gillum added a positive perception subscale to ensure the representation of all views and keep from biasing the results.[32] The scoring scale for each subscale ranged from one (strongly disagree) to six (strongly agree); a mean score greater than three indicated some agreement with the image.[33]

- 48 percent of the sample endorsed the Jezebel stereotype;
- 71 percent of the sample endorsed the Matriarch stereotype;
- 94 percent of the sample endorsed positive beliefs about African American women.[34]

Gillum's research study is limited in geographic location; however, it argues that social and cultural variables influence IPV in the African

27. Gillum, "Exploring the Link," 64–86.
28. Gillum, "Exploring the Link."
29. West, "Mammy, Sapphire, and Jezebel," 458–66.
30. Gillum, "Exploring the Link."
31. Gillum, "Exploring the Link."
32. Gillum, "Exploring the Link."
33. Gillum, "Exploring the Link."
34. Gillum, "Exploring the Link."

American community, with implications for developing IPV interventions that are culturally appropriate for African Americans.

Mass media and popular culture perpetuate racially disparaging narratives and visuals portraying African American women as highly sexual, "welfare queens," "pornographic video stars," and "bad Black girls," who are dangerous particularly in mainstream rap videos.[35] These stereotypical images are inherited from colonization and slavery, as indicated by the white-male-dominated culture in America. The societal promotion of negative African American personas endorses these negative images.[36]

A study participant in my research shared her early childhood struggle with negative media images and stereotypes, stating, " . . . why don't I just emulate what they say I am? Why don't I be bad? Why don't I be fast? Why don't I just meet a stranger and be promiscuous because these are the things that I was taught or told from the very people who were supposed to protect and love me and not necessarily my parent . . . "[37] These disparaging images are internalized in society and have a detrimental psychological impact on how African American women and girls see themselves. Risk factors for developing low self-esteem and being impacted by IPV, then, also include institutional racism and internalized racism.[38]

The Black Church

The Black church has consistently served as a steadfast source of hope and support for the African American community. Pew Research Center states that 79 percent of African Americans self-identify as Christian.[39] The Black church is where many African Americans turn to for a prophetic voice during times of crisis and to deal with social injustices and inequalities that impact the community. It is where members turn first to seek help, which signifies the importance of religious interventions for IPV.[40] About 70 percent of the congregation in the African American church are women.[41] However, African American women represent only 8.3 percent of

---

35. Richardson, "She Was Workin like Foreal," 789–809.
36. Richardson, "She Was Workin like Foreal, 789–809."
37. Study Participant 3.
38. Brice-Baker, "Domestic Violence."
39. Masci. "5 Facts."
40. Williams and Becker, "Treatment Programs," 287–96.
41. Abernethy, "Women's Leadership."

the 433,000 US clergy, with predominately men having senior leadership roles.[42] Since 87.1 percent of currently employed pastors in the US are men, that means only 12.9 percent of all pastors are women.[43]

Williams and Jenkins surveyed Black pastors and leaders nationally to determine their awareness of IPV and victims and how they respond to them. The data indicate that pastors and church leaders underestimate the number of members who are victims; there is a lack of sermons and teaching on domestic violence; and clergy can implement harmful interventions.[44] Therefore, the church may want to merge psychological, emotional, and spiritual realms to address trauma and IPV.

This work makes the argument for the implementation of trauma-informed theology as a building block for the development of an African American culturally competent trauma-informed care IPV curriculum with biblical principles as an intervention tool to increase the awareness of IPV in African American women among the clergy and laity. The curriculum attempts to open communication channels within and outside the church to discuss trauma and IPV to inform interventions and prevention strategies practical for implementation within existing church programming for women, children, and family ministries.

Historical Overview of the Pentecostal Ministry Context

Imagine, just for a moment, stepping into the heart of the African American community not simply as a pastor, teacher, or leader, but as a thoughtful observer. Like a cultural scientist, you're peering into what I call a "cultural petri dish." You're not just seeing people living their lives; you're witnessing generations of belief, tradition, resilience, and pain. You see faith practices passed down like sacred heirlooms, rituals that give rhythm to daily life, and histories carried in bodies and memories. You also see the hidden, often unspoken, realities of how culture shapes how people love, speak, worship, and, sometimes, suffer.

Now, let's zoom in. Let's focus on a deeply troubling and often overlooked thread in this larger story: the urgent experience of African American women navigating IPV within Pentecostal ministry. This is where my research begins. Not just with the visible harm but also with the hidden

---

42. Smarr, Disbennett-Lee, and Hakim, "Gender and Race," 377.
43. Zippia, "Pastor Demographic and Statistics in the U.S."
44. Williams and Jenkins, "A Survey of Black Churches," 21–38.

roots. Why is violence showing up in sacred spaces meant for refuge, healing, and restoration? How is it sustained? What keeps it hidden? What allows it to persist? Why isn't it being talked about more openly?

As I listened, studied, and prayed through this work, quiet patterns became insistent. Again and again, I encountered the same core influences shaping how the church, particularly in Pentecostal settings, understands and responds to IPV. These include the powerful Day of Pentecost, that foundational moment in faith. But they also include the enduring wounds of colonialism and slavery, the structure of institutional Pentecostalism, our interpretive lens (what we call Pentecostal hermeneutics, the method of interpreting Scripture within the Pentecostal tradition), and our understanding of the Pentecostal Trinity.

But these aren't just theological reference points. They are threads woven into the culture of the church. Together, they form a tapestry, and when I looked closely, I noticed a pattern shaped by patriarchy. Patriarchy is not always intentional but present nonetheless, living in our leadership models, our teaching, the way we form disciples, and, perhaps most painfully, in the silences surrounding suffering. These silences, often born out of a lack of understanding or discomfort, contribute to the perpetuation of violence.

These threads help explain how even a Spirit-filled, Bible-centered church can miss or misunderstand the cries of women experiencing violence. And that realization calls us, as leaders, into reflection and action. Your role in this—your influence, your voice—is crucial.

The Birth of the Church on the Day of Pentecost

According to the Bible, every nation and culture was represented in Jerusalem on the Day of Pentecost in A.D. 33.[45] "Parthians, Medes, and Elamites; residents of Mesopotamia, Judea and Cappadocia, Pontus and Asia, Phrygia and Pamphylia, Egypt and the parts of Libya near Cyrene; visitors from Rome (both Jews and converts to Judaism); Cretans and Arabs—we hear them declaring the wonders of God in our tongues" (Acts 2:9–11, NIV). It is imperative to emphasize that representatives from the continent of Africa were present on that glorious day. It is far too common to overlook or undervalue Africa's contribution to Christianity and the early church,

---

45. Humphreys and Waddington, "The Jewish Calendar," 331–51.

which may be due to colonialism. However, many early church fathers and theologians in the first through third centuries AD were African:[46,47]

- Augustine, Bishop of Hippo—Algeria, North Africa
- Tertullian, Lawyer/Apologist—Carthage, North Africa
- Cyprian, Carthage Bishop—Carthage, North Africa
- Perpetua, Christian Writer/Martyr (The Passion of Saints Perpetua and Felicity, first Christian text written by an African woman)—Carthage, North Africa
- Athanasius of Alexandria, Egyptian Bishop—Egypt, North Africa
- Origen of Alexandria, Theologian—Egypt, North Africa

Then, it can be ascertained that enslaved Africans brought their Christianity with them as they were transported through the Middle Passage to the shores of the US. In 1619, Bishop Manuel Bautista Soares, a local Roman Catholic, penned a letter expressing his disapproval of the abduction of more than 4,000 African Christians from Ndongo in west-central Africa by slave traders.[48] This justifies creating an IPV intervention curriculum for clergy that is culturally suitable for African American descendants of the African diaspora because it is inclusive of the enslaved African experience and acknowledges the African Christian heritage, which is applicable in a ministry context.

The Second Great Awakening

The church's Second Great Awakening (1795–1835) was a Protestant revival, mostly among Methodist and Baptist churches in America, that emerged at the height of the American slave trade. The movement had the following characteristics: abolitionist sentiments, emotional appeal, exuberant religion, spirituality for enslaved people, and religious body movements that resonated with native Africanism. This movement focused on the experience of conversion rather than intellectual capacity. The pretext for this could be Calvinism theology, which possibly supported slavery by the Puritans.

46. Oden, *How Africa Shaped the Christian Mind*, 14, 45, 49, 51.
47. Salisbury, "Perpetua."
48. Daniels, "1619 and The Arrival of African Christianity."

As noted by Estrelda Y. Alexander, Calvinist theology fits the structure of the institution of slavery; the precepts are that some Blacks were predestined by God to be enslaved, and some whites were destined to be masters.[49] However, the revivals promoted racial openness and gender inclusiveness. The revivals encouraged interracial fellowship and allowed Black preachers and laypersons to minister among white congregations. In 1788, Lemuel Haynes became the first Black pastor to lead a white church, and he received an honorary degree. He also was the first Black person to publish a book, titled *Black Preacher to White America: The Collected Writings of Lemuel 1774–1833*.[50] The revival also opened doors for women, allowing them to take their rightful place in ministry. A few African American women preachers during that era that advanced Holiness and Pentecostal churches are:[51]

- Jarena Lee (1783–1864)—the first African American woman to preach in the African Methodist Episcopal Church.
- Sojourner Truth (Isabella Baumfree) (1797–1883)—a Black abolitionist, co-founder of Kingston Methodist Church.
- Amanda Berry Smith (1837–1915)—an African Methodist Episcopal Church preacher. She became the first Black woman international evangelist in 1878, evangelizing in Europe, Asia, and Africa for twelve years.
- Lucy Farrow (1851–1911)—a Black pastor in 1905 of a Holiness Church in Houston, Texas. She worked for Charles Parham as a governess to his children; in 1906, William Seymore asked her to teach glossolalia at the Azusa Street Revival. Her ministry was especially fruitful in the southern US, Liberia, and West Africa.

Arlene M. Sanchez Walsh, in her book *Pentecostals in America*, argues that John Alexander Dowie, Charles Parham, Aimee Semple McPherson, and A.A. Allen are responsible for branding American Pentecostalism in nineteenth-century America, and white Pentecostal leaders in historical narratives have often overlooked Willam J. Seymore's contribution.[52] Walsh's argument allows Seymore, an African American Holy preacher

---

49. Alexander, *Black Fire*, 64.
50. Anyabwile, "This Black Pastor Led a White Church—in 1788."
51. Perry, "10 Awesome Women Pastors from History."
52. Sanchez Walsh, *Pentecostals in America*, xxii, 14.

who led the Azusa Street Revival, to enter the scene. Seymore's Azusa Street Revival (1906–1915) is our modern-day example of Pentecostalism worldwide. A significant portion of the attendees of this religious revival consisted of individuals who had previously been enslaved or were descendants of enslaved individuals.

James S. Tinney states that the Pentecostal movement has roots in Africa and "thrives" in the African diaspora.[53] These features of Pentecostalism traveled with enslaved Africans through the Middle Passage:

> universal belief in a supreme being, a pervasive sense of the reality of the spirit world, blurring of lines between the sacred and profane, practical use of religion in all of life, surrender of excessive individualism for community solidarity, reverence for ancestors and their symbolic communal presence, greater involvement of women in ritual and community leadership, and creative use of rhythm, singing, and dance in life and worship has had implications for African spirituality.[54]

Therefore, Tinney suggests that Pentecostal expressions such as music, dance, drumming, and speaking in tongues reflect African spiritual traditions. Though rooted in ancient Christian practices, Pentecostal theology may be connected to African philosophical thought.[55] Tinney considers Pentecostalism "truly African" in its worship style, the doctrine of faith, practices, and organizational structure, which includes spirits, sorcery, and eschatology.[56] Pentecostalism did not require enslaved Africans or free Africans (Blacks) to forsake their indigenous religious rituals. Conversely, it allowed individuals to integrate their African perspective, cultural legacy, and spiritual sense of self inside the Pentecostalism paradigm. Africanism is intrinsic, innate, and indigenous to African people. It indwells in their spirit as the Holy Spirit in Christians, expressed in all facets of the church and the community. Africanism is a feature of Pentecostalism that cannot be separated from mainline Pentecostalism.

The climax of the Azusa Street Revival, when congregations had interracial diversity, equity, and inclusion in the congregation and church leadership, was the marquee of Pentecostalism. The Second Awakening ushered in the Holiness and Pentecostal movements with its signature hallmark of

---

53. Tinney, "The Blackness of Pentecostalism," 27, quoted in Alexander, *Black Fire*.
54. Alexander, *Black Fire*, 31.
55. Tinney, "The Blackness of Pentecostalism," 27, in Alexander, *Black Fire*.
56. Tinney, "The Blackness of Pentecostalism," 27, in Alexander, *Black Fire*.

interracial fellowship and church leadership, providing both Black preachers and women an opportunity to preach. The sermons were often messages of holiness and sanctification, resulting in the social consciousness of the congregates. However, outside of the revival, worshippers encountered threats and violence, given the social milieu of structural and systemic racism, leading to homogeneous churches. "Singing the Lord's Song in a Strange Land" (Ps 137:4) is a fitting description of the lived experience of Blacks in predominantly white Pentecostal congregations in the past and present day. David Harrell reported that in 1958, half a million Blacks were affiliated with white denominations in segregated congregations, and eight thousand attended church in predominately white congregations.[57] He also reported that in 1971, the status quo did not change, and in 1990, only forty thousand African Americans were in predominately white Pentecostal denominations.[58] Today's homogeneous Black church, and other homogeneous churches that serve specific ethnic groups, emphasizes the need for clergy to have access to culturally sensitive ministry IPV intervention tools. These tools should effectively convey the cultural context of the congregation in order to facilitate practical applications.

The Aftermath of Slavery on Pentecostalism

According to Gaston Espinosa, "scholars agree that Pentecostalism was shaped by nineteenth-century slave religion, revivalism, Black and white Holiness theology, the Keswick movement, the Reformed idea of power for Christian living, dispensational premillennialism, and divine healing movement."[59] Within these theological settings in America, slavery was abolished in 1865 at the end of the Civil War. However, other social and cultural events influenced racial relations after the war, such as Reconstruction, the formation of the Ku Klux Klan, segregation, and the Great Migration (upward mobility for Blacks). Segregation laws institutionalized racial segregation of Blacks and whites, relegating them to "separate but equal" divisions. Charles H. Mason and Charles P. Jones established the first Black Holiness Pentecostal denomination in 1897—The Church of God in Christ in Mississippi.[60] It could be suggested that white Pentecostals perhaps

---

57. Alexander, *Black Fire*, 251–52.
58. Alexander, *Black Fire*, 251–52.
59. Espinosa, *William J. Seymour and the Origins of Global Pentecostalism*, 42.
60. Sanchez Walsh, *Pentecostals in America*, 42.

exhibited social and cultural norms embedded in a patriarchal society that favors white men. It is important to note that Blacks in these white Pentecostal spaces were either members of primarily white or multiracial congregations or predominately Black congregations led by white pastors. Unfortunately, Blacks in these settings were invisible and restricted from coming together on racial and political issues.

It is within this culture of patriarchy that Black men are allowed to vote before white women as their white male counterparts granted to them by the Fifteenth Amendment in the US Constitution in 1870 after the Civil War. It seems as if Black men had found their voices in society by engaging in the process of assimilation and acculturation, aligning themselves with white men in society, yet not achieving true equality as they faced systemic barriers and discrimination. Neither white women nor Black women were given voting privileges, only men. During the pre–Civil War era of the 1800s, white women actively advocated for suffrage as they sought to attain the right to vote. Following the war's conclusion, Black women actively participated in the Suffrage movement, advocating for their right to vote and making significant contributions to the cause. In the meantime, women continued founding Pentecostal denominations during the 1900s–1920s:[61,62]

- Mary Magdalena Tate (1903)—Church of the Living God Pillar and Ground of the Truth
- Florence Crawford (1907)—Apostolic Faith Mission in Portland, Oregon
- Aimee Semple McPherson (1923)—International Church of the Foursquare Gospel
- Ida Robinson (1924)—Mount Sinai Holy Church of America (Parent Body United House of Prayer)
- Maria Woodworth-Etter (1924)—Woodworth Tabernacle in Indianapolis (present-day name Lakeview Church)
- Currie Gury (1929)—Kings Apostle Holiness Church

The Nineteenth Amendment to the US Constitution, which granted women the right to vote, passed in 1919 and was ratified in 1920. It can be inferred that women who were advocating for their suffrage rights

---

61. Langford, "Feminism and Leadership," 69–79.
62. Alexander, *Black Fire*, 342.

were challenging androcentric systems that upheld the "Cult of True Womanhood,"[63] a concept rooted in male-dominated ideology. This ideology asserts that the only acceptable form of womanhood is one characterized by piety, submissiveness, and a primary focus on domestic and family matters.[64] It is at this juncture that the Pentecostal ministry context considers patriarchal systems and the intersectionality of women to examine risk factors that may prevent clergy from realizing, recognizing, and responding to IPV, leading to them unintentionally retraumatizing women survivors of IPV in a ministry context.

Intersectionality

An in-depth understanding of how intersectionality operates in the lives of African American women is essential for analyzing the risk factors linked to IPV within this demographic. Intersectionality helps us understand that people don't experience life through just one lens. A person's race, gender, class, age, ability, or faith can overlap in ways that make them more vulnerable to harm or being overlooked. When these parts of who we are meet systems that are already unequal, it can deepen the pain. As faith leaders, recognizing this helps us better see the whole person in front of us and serve with deeper compassion, justice, and care.

Kimberlé Crenshaw created the intersectionality theory in 1989. This theory takes critical thinking beyond segmenting race and gender and pivots to the multiplicity of factors to consider in social and cultural contexts. Figure 3 provides an illustration of intersectionality and the crossroads of interconnections. This theory considers all ignored diverse identities, in addition to the socially excluded, to understand oppressive systems in a person or group. The intersectionality hypothesis can help identify social justice problems that manifest where social and cultural identities converge, leading to systemic oppression, discrimination, and violence against women.

Given this framework, examining Pentecostal ministry environments requires analyzing how institutional structures—particularly patriarchal hierarchies—impact the convergence of gender, race, and religious identity in ways that may perpetuate harm.

---

63. History.com, "Women's Suffrage."
64. History.com, "Women's Suffrage."

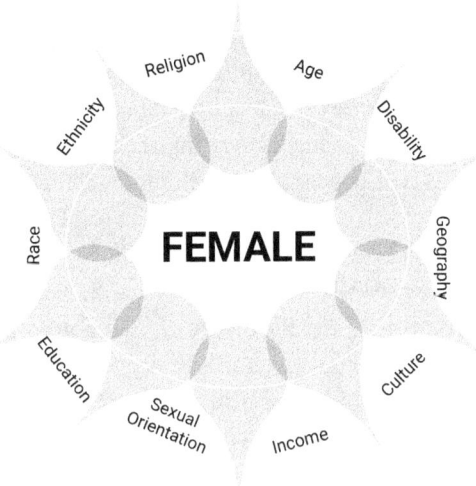

Figure 3. Intersectionality

Risk Factors within Pentecostalism

The Patriarchy

While a patriarchal framework is not universally applicable, it is prevalent in societies across the globe.[65] Male supremacy is cultivated in patriarchal societies to uphold authority in society, government, institutions, and economic structures. The system is gender-based and has a bias toward men, giving them preferential treatment over women that could result in gender inequity and oppression for women in their interpersonal and intimate relationships.

The argument that the Bible supports a patriarchal social structure has been a topic of debate.[66] However, biblical theology does not support this claim. Since both men and women were made in the image of God, it can be argued that they are not inferior to one another but equal. As noted in Gen 1:27, "So God created mankind in his image, in the image of God he created them; male and female he created them."

---

65. Encyclopedia Britannica, "Patriarchy."
66. Bourna, "Is the Bible 'Patriarchal?"

Weingreen argues that the Bible provides the first women's civil rights case study in the story told in Num 27:1–11, which recounts the story of the daughters (Mahlah, Noa, Hoglah, Milcah, and Tirzah) of Zelophehad. This narrative might be interpreted as a legal proceeding that involves two critical social and cultural concepts meeting at the intersection between the hierarchical structure of the family and the financial consequences of inheritance law.[67] The case requires analyzing the social and cultural context, including patriarchal ordering and inheritance law.[68]

The daughters were descendants of Manasseh from Joseph. Their father died in the wilderness, and the discourse is about how they can receive their father's allotment of land, given that they are brotherless, endangering the family's chances of gaining any land inheritance and further marginalizing the women into destitution. Schmidt's article, "Strategic Leadership as Modeled by the Daughters of Zelophehad," affirms that the culture of the Israelites was patriarchal, prioritizing male leadership and male successors with family life centered around the senior male; children and women were considered commodities, and women were reliant on their husbands or fathers.[69] Within this patriarchal milieu of the Israelites migrating to the Promised Land, the daughters of Zelophehad made their case at the tent of meetings as led by Moses and his male leadership team. Within this patrilineal society, principles outlined in Deut 21:15–17 dictate that social hierarchy and inheritance rights are reserved for males.[70] These women showed courageous faith to advocate for their family and their rights.

Moses sought guidance from the Lord, considering the mandates of the social order and the law governing inheritance within their cultural context. Moses received divine confirmation from the Lord that the daughters should be entitled to their father's estate, irrespective of prevailing customs. Women's legal rights to inherit their father's estate and property without a male counterpart put into practice in this case. This ruling from the Lord in favor of these women upholds the line of reasoning that patriarchy is a manufactured idea in a sinful world.

However, the patriarchal system continued, as evidenced in Num 36:1–13. According to this passage, the five daughters of Zelophehad were

---

67. Weingreen, "The Case of the Daughters of Zelophchad," 518–22.
68. Schmidt, "Strategic Leadership," 102–112.
69. Schmidt, "Strategic Leadership."
70. Keil and Delitzsch Old Testament Commentary, "Deuteronomy 21."

legally obligated to marry men from their clan in order to preserve the family's inherited property within the bloodline.

As Pentecostals, we too must acknowledge how a patriarchal dogma can influence the organizational structure, hermeneutics, and trinity theology within Pentecostalism. We must also take this a step further and understand how these affect women, if Pentecostalism is to advance social justice and give voice to the voiceless in intimate relationships.

Institutional Pentecostalism Negates the Prophetic Call for Diversity, Equity, and Inclusion

Pentecostalism in the early 1900s not only opened the doors for women to operate in their calling to ministry and spiritual gifts, but it also opened the doors of diversity, equity, and inclusion (DEI) of all races to come together to worship and praise God, as modeled at the Azusa Street Revival from 1906 to 1915. There were three prophetic interpretations of Pentecostalism between 1901 and 1920 that were responsible for initial gender equality within the denomination:[71]

1. The call to ministry was not gender-specific
2. The community's affirmation of the call was based on their recognition of the individual's charm
3. The community's eschatological belief is that they were experiencing the latter rain (Joel 2:23), in which your sons *and daughters* will prophesy (Joel 2:28; emphasis added)

If the Pentecostal movement had adhered to these three principles, then the influence of patriarchal systems in society may not have entered classical Pentecostalism.

The empowerment of women's voices in Pentecostal church leadership started to wane after the 1920s as the Pentecostal religious community adapted to the social and cultural contextualization of patriarchal institutions. To various degrees, the movement had shifted from a prophetic call to a priestly call, giving men leadership control. "With the centralization of ecclesiastical authority, only district councils officially could grant ministerial ordination."[72]

---

71. Barfoot et al., "Prophetic vs. Priestly Religion."
72. Barfoot et al., "Prophetic vs. Priestly Religion."

Women and the disadvantaged classes were paramount to the growth of Pentecostalism in the religious community nationally and globally. They could be teachers, ministers, associate ministers, evangelists, and missionaries, but ordination was reserved only for men as priestly duties for elders, pastors, and bishops. It can be inferred that this is subject to men's authority, not God's. Within this framework, institutions restricted women's leadership with limited access to ordination, as many Pentecostal churches aligned themselves with a fundamentalist view of gender-specific roles in the church.[73] In Edith L. Blumhofer's, "Restoring the Faith: The Assemblies of God, Pentecostalism, and American Culture," from 1993 (quoted in Longford 2017), John G. Lake stated, "The denomination was commendably efficient but was most emphatically not Pentecostal . . . the movement had drifted clear away from a true scriptural Pentecost idea."[74]

It is also essential to observe that in 1914, the Church of God in Christ (COGIC) divided along racial lines, resulting in the Assemblies of God (white ministers) and COGIC (Black ministers) continuing as founded by Charles H. Mason. The two churches may have split on racial issues and leadership; however, they agreed that the priestly duties of elders and bishops are only ascribed to men in the religious community. In 1935, the Assemblies of God made priestly duties available to women as equal to men; nevertheless, upward mobility for women was limited.[75] These two church models of the organizational structure of Pentecostalism as constructed by men have influenced Pentecostal religious communities globally, since they were planted at the genesis of classical Pentecostalism, which influences various categories within the movement (i.e., Oneness, Charismatics, and Independents).

Janet Meyers Everts says in *Brokenness as the Centre of a Woman's Ministry*, "Given the patriarchalism and sexism that [Pentecostal] women have endured, they have been the most broken and therefore the most receptive to the infilling and empowerment of the Holy Spirit."[76] This observation suggests the presence of strained interpersonal interactions between individuals of different genders within the setting of a Pentecostal ministry. This finding highlights the importance of implementing an intervention curriculum on IPV specifically tailored for clergy within the framework

---

73. Langford, "Feminism and Leadership."
74. Langford, "Feminism and Leadership."
75. Robeck, "Women in Pentecostal Movement."
76. Langford, "Feminism and Leadership."

of a Pentecostal ministry. Additionally, it highlights the importance of increasing the representation of women in senior leadership positions within this ministry, ultimately leading to the achievement of gender equality.

Pentecostal Hermeneutics

Pentecostal hermeneutics may freeze women out of senior church leadership roles and prevent clergy from realizing, recognizing, responding, and resisting retraumatizing women victim-survivors of IPV in the church and the community. The two types of Pentecostal hermeneutics are articulated and unarticulated. Pentecostal hermeneutics "adopt[ed] a system of interpretation heavily slanted toward rationalism and [it] has little room for the role of the Holy Spirit."[77] It is suggested that women in this community of faith are supported in operating in the prophetic; however, the women are expected to work within a patriarchal social and cultural context.

Articulated Pentecostal hermeneutics refers to the scholarly practice of analyzing and interpreting the Bible.[78] "This hermeneutic reflects on the traditions and ethos presented within the Pentecostal tradition to appreciate the role of the Holy Spirit and religious experience in interpreting the Bible."[79] Unarticulated Pentecostalism, however, happens in the pews, church, and spiritual community as the members are engaged in forming and developing this framework, consciously or not, in a patriarchal environment.[80] The contextualization of women in traditional roles in the community influences them to be submissive to men at home and in the church.

How these two Pentecostal hermeneutics interpret scriptures demotes women in the church and the community. A literal reading may marginalize women; this interpretation does not consider the historical context.[81] Proof-texting is the second interpretation strategy that may push women to the periphery of society in the church and the community. Gabaiste states, "Proof-texting refers to the art of using and harmonizing a few biblical texts to support an argument without considering how those texts relate to the Bible as a whole."[82] In proof-texting, church doctrines and policies for the

---

77. Gabaitse, "Pentecostal Hermeneutics and the Marginalization of Women," 1–12.
78. Gabaitse, "Pentecostal Hermeneutics."
79. Gabaitse, "Pentecostal Hermeneutics."
80. Gabaitse, "Pentecostal Hermeneutics."
81. Gabaitse, "Pentecostal Hermeneutics."
82. Gabaitse, "Pentecostal Hermeneutics."

religious community are created using a stand-alone verse. For example, when interpreted literally, Gen 2:22–24, 1 Cor 11:3, 1 Cor 14:35, 1 Tim 2:9, and Eph 5:22 are all oppressive to women. They take away her voice to speak truth to power and take away the community's fight for social justice for IPV. Thus, these Pentecostal biblical interpretation strategies may harm women and create an environment that encourages violence against women.

A literal and proof-texting illustration of Eph 5:22–24 image is provided below.

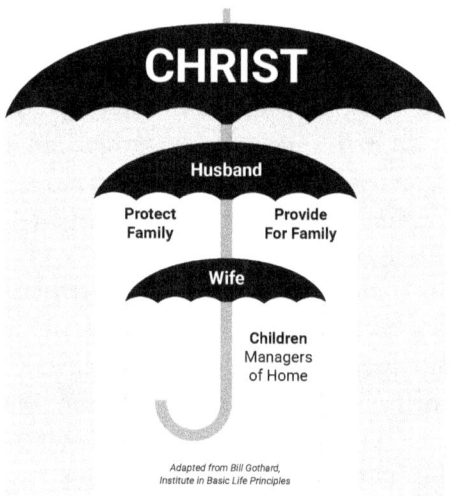

Figure 4. The Umbrella of Protection

Pentecostal Trinity Theology

The doctrine of the Trinity in Pentecostalism further disregards women in the religious community. The argument is that there is a hierarchy within the Trinity based on subordination in the following order: God the Father, God the Son, and God the Holy Spirit.[83] This theological premise is supposed to be projected on men, women, and children, with their physiological differences used to position men as head of the household, followed by women and then children, yielding an androcentric perspective. This theology is not a universally shared viewpoint of all Pentecostals; many believe the Trinity is a relationship of equality, coexistence, and mutuality.

83. Gabaitse, "Pentecostal Hermeneutics."

However, the prevalence of IPV within churches and communities could be reduced if Pentecostal theology more fully embraced the mutuality and equality modeled in the Trinity—honoring women as co-bearers of God's image rather than marginalizing them through distorted doctrines of subordination.

Case Study

There appears to be very little research specifically on Pentecostal theology and IPV. However, I found a study of Pentecostal theology and gender-based violence (GBV), including IPV. The United Nations defines violence against women as "any act of gender-based violence that results in physical, sexual, or mental harm or suffering to women, including threats of such acts, coercion, and arbitrary deprivation of liberty."[84] Nomatter Sande studied Pentecostal theology and GBV in Zimbabwe within the context of the Apostolic Faith Mission (AFM) Pentecostal ministry. The premise of that study is that the institution of marriage within the framework of AFM Pentecostalism theology enables GBV. AFM Pentecostal theology perpetrates GBV against women through its social and cultural context within the religious community.

Pentecostal churches often do not recognize GBV because it is "wrapped in the aura of love presented in the marriage institution."[85] Most of the members in churches are women; however, despite their more significant numbers, there is no solution to the problem of GBV. The study claims that the emotional view of love, marriage, and family that women hold makes them susceptible to GBV.[86] The study employs a theoretical framework that draws upon a post-feminist viewpoint to examine the structural aspects of marital institutions. Additionally, it incorporates intersectionality theology to advocate for the promotion of liberation, reconciliation, and peace within the context of marriage. The study included a sample of seventy married women who identified as AFM. These participants were administered a questionnaire designed to gather information about their experiences with sexuality, intimacy, and violence. The study also involved observing participants engaging in AFM sermons, marriage seminars, and counseling sessions.

---

84. United Nations, "Declaration on the Elimination of Violence."
85. Sande, "Pentecostal Theology and Gender-based Violence," 1–12.
86. Sande, "Pentecostal Theology and Gender-based Violence."

In this study, Sande observed that issues and themes around GBV "were skirted around, and most teachings and participants were very reticent to broach this topic."[87] GBV is rooted in Zimbabwe's history; rape is used as a weapon, like an arsenal for artillery when the country is at war. GBV is embedded in a culture that is fueled by a patriarchal society and interwoven in the church culture "in how the marriage is conceptualized in both the African indigenous culture and Pentecostal theology."[88] The primary focus for marriage in indigenous culture is to extend the family's lineage and financial stability; it is reverence, and the ancestral spirits are evoked to participate in the ceremony. In Pentecostal theology, marriage is sacred, represents the union between man and woman, and can only be resolved by death.

At the core, the AFM response to GBV is a theological issue. According to Sande, spiritual gifts from the Holy Spirit, such as miracles, prayer, and fasting, create a pretense that GBV does not exist in the congregation. "Even victims often deny the reality of abuse in the faith and hope God would intervene to stop it."[89] The AFM does not have a solution to GBV. It struggles to define a remedy because of its literal reading of the Bible. The study suggests that AFM theology legitimizes GBV because it teaches that suffering is a gateway to spiritual elevation. The AFM teaches that women should be submissive to their husband, a potential risk factor that grooms women for GBV.[90]

Suppose GBV is brought to the attention of church leadership. In that case, an intervention will be through the internal grievance processes of the AFM, as guidelines are informed by 1 Cor 6:1–18, and not brought to the attention of the police.[91] Other intervention strategies to address GBV when attempted to be resolved in the church are the AFM rituals of prayer and fasting.[92] The study's findings show that Zimbabwe's AFM needs alternative solutions for GBV. Its Pentecostal theological frameworks are rooted in the indigenous culture of a patriarchal society. They have an unarticulated and literal interpretation of biblical scriptures that favor the superiority of men over women. The study concluded that there is no safe or public space for

---

87. Sande, "Pentecostal Theology and Gender-based Violence."
88. Sande, "Pentecostal Theology and Gender-based Violence."
89. Sande, "Pentecostal Theology and Gender-based Violence."
90. Sande, "Pentecostal Theology and Gender-based Violence."
91. Sande, "Pentecostal Theology and Gender-based Violence."
92. Sande, "Pentecostal Theology and Gender-based Violence."

conversations about GBV in the AFM and the religious community. Even though the scope of this study is small, it has global implications.

There is an alternative way to address IPV in Pentecostal ministry: one rooted in the Gospel and grounded in grace. A path is beginning to unfold, and it calls us, as clergy, to lead with greater discernment and spiritual courage. By embracing trauma-informed theology, we empower ourselves and our churches with a renewed vision. One who sees with the eyes of Christ hears the cries that have long gone unheard and responds not with defensiveness but with compassion, clarity, and conviction.

This approach does more than name the problem. It invites us into the sacred work of healing. It shines light into the corners we've been taught to avoid. It opens space for truth to be spoken in rooms where silence once reigned. Perhaps most importantly, it offers a beacon of hope that our churches can truly become sanctuaries, not just in word but in action.

If we are to reduce the presence of IPV in our congregations and raise true awareness among our leadership, we must begin by reexamining the theological systems we have inherited. Chapter 2 will explore alternative frameworks rethinking institutional Pentecostalism, reconsidering our interpretive lens, and reflecting more deeply on our theology of the Trinity. These shifts do not depart from our faith but return to its core where love, justice, and truth dwell.

The time for silence has passed. The time for a faithful, informed, and Spirit-sensitive response is now. And it begins with us.

2

Recognize

As Pentecostal leaders and ministers, we are called to a deeper understanding of how our faith intersects with culture, politics, and history, particularly in the context of Africa. Pentecostalism in Africa, and what we call *African Pentecostalism*, represents a dynamic and complex relationship shaped not only by the outpouring of the Spirit but also by the enduring legacies of colonization and the struggles of postcolonial identity.

In examining this relationship, we are invited to engage with what some scholars call an *African Pentecostal Political Philosophy*. This emerging framework, in simpler terms, is a way of understanding how Pentecostalism in Africa has responded to and been shaped by a host of intersecting forces such as secularism, citizenship, poverty, economic instability, race, ethnicity, gender, ecumenism, and interfaith dynamics. It challenges us to see how theology and politics are not separate realms but deeply entwined, often shaping one another in visible and invisible ways.

Pentecostalism's rise across the African continent since the 1950s and 1960s was more than a spiritual awakening; it was also a social and political statement. Many Africans moved away from mainline mission churches, embracing Pentecostal and Charismatic expressions of Christianity that honored their own spiritual worldview and cultural identity. This movement birthed African Independent Churches and reinvigorated the local voice in Christian faith and practice.

According to the Pew Research Center's most recent research on the topic, conducted in 2006, Christianity remains the world's largest religious group, and Pentecostalism continues to expand rapidly across Africa and the global South. This global expansion tells us clearly that African Pentecostalism is not just a religious phenomenon but a growing spiritual, cultural, and political force of which we are an integral part. It offers a powerful platform for self-agency, community transformation, and prophetic engagement in the public square particularly for the marginalized and the poor.

As we journey through this chapter, we will explore how Pentecostalism can serve as a spiritual movement and a vehicle for justice, renewal, and global democratic participation. This is a moment for the church—especially Pentecostal leaders—to consider how we can faithfully steward this influence. It's a responsibility that we must take seriously, ensuring that our actions always honor Christ, empower communities, and engage the complexities of the world around us. Below are charts depicting Christianity in Africa, religious groups, and the world Christian population.

CHRISTIANITY IN AFRICA

	1900		1970		1990		2005	
	In millions	As % of total population	In millions	As % of total population	In millions	As % of total population	In millions	As % of total population
Christians	10	9%	144	40%	276	45%	411	46%
Catholics	2	2	45	13	91	15	147	17
Protestants, Anglicans and Independents	2	2	53	15	162	26	253	29

Source: World Christian Encyclopedia (2001) and World Christian Database (2006)[1]

Figure 5. Christianity in Africa

---

1. Pew Research Center, "Christianity in Africa."

World Christian Population by Region, 2010 and 2050

	YEAR	REGION'S TOTAL POPULATION	REGION'S CHRISTIAN POPULATION	% CHRISTIAN IN REGION
Europe	2010	742,550,000	553,280,000	74.5%
	2050	696,330,000	454,090,000	65.2
Latin America–Caribbean	2010	590,080,000	531,280,000	90.0
	2050	748,620,000	665,500,000	88.9
Sub-Saharan Africa	2010	822,730,000	517,320,000	62.9
	2050	1,899,960,000	1,112,390,000	58.5
Asia-Pacific	2010	4,054,940,000	287,100,000	7.1
	2050	4,937,900,000	381,200,000	7.7
North America	2010	344,530,000	266,630,000	77.4
	2050	435,420,000	286,710,000	65.8
Middle East–North Africa	2010	341,020,000	12,710,000	3.7
	2050	588,960,000	18,180,000	3.1

Source: The Future of World Religions: Population Growth Projections, 2010-2050
Population estimates are rounded to the nearest 10,000. Percentages are calculated from unrounded numbers.

PEW RESEARCH CENTER

Figure 6. World Christian Population by Region, 2010 and 2050

Exploring Africa's potential role in identifying alternative approaches to mitigating the intersectionality of IPV risk factors associated with clergy's inability to acknowledge, understand, address, and resist retraumatizing Black women who have experienced abuse within Pentecostalism and religious communities is of utmost importance.

What is the rationale for directing attention toward Africa? The early African church fathers and theologians had a crucial role in developing early Christianity and forming Christian worldviews. Additionally, numerous studies have provided evidence suggesting that both the African American community and women in the African diaspora exhibit higher rates of IPV in both the United States and Africa. The epidemic of IPV has significant global repercussions on women worldwide. Figure 5 provides an illustration of the victims per 100,000 female population as a reference.

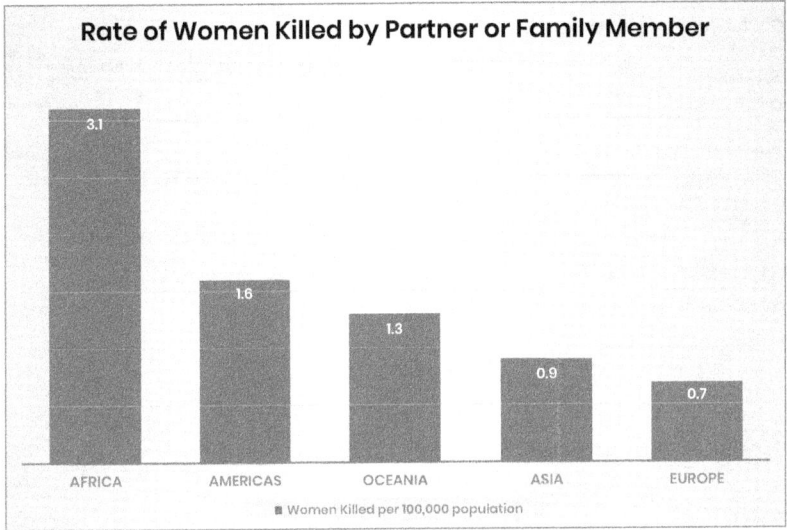

Figure 7. Rate of Women Killed by Partner or Family Members per 100,000 Population[2]

Examining IPV within the Pentecostal ministry setting requires considering global IPV data since Pentecostalism is, as of the last survey, the fastest-growing religion globally. Approximately 25 percent of the contemporary Christian population identifies as Pentecostals or charismatics.[3] It is imperative to convey that both groups subscribe to the spiritual endowments the Holy Spirit bestows. Additionally, it is worth noting that 25 percent of Christians in the United States self-identify as followers of the Pentecostal tradition.[4] With what we know about the prevalence of IPV in the United States, one thing is clear: there are victims and survivors of IPV sitting in the pews.

2. United Nations, "Home, the Most Dangerous Place for Women."
3. Pew Research Center, "The New Face of Global Christianity."
4. Barrick, "Survey: 1 in 4 U.S. Christians Identify as Pentecostal."

Christians by Movement

Movements	ESTIMATED NUMBER	PERCENTAGE OF TOTAL WORLD POPULATION	PERCENTAGE OF WORLD CHRISTIAN POPULATION
Pentecostal	279,080,000	4.0%	12.8%
Charismatic	304,990,000	4.4	14.0
Pentecostal & Charismatic together	**584,080,000**	**8.5**	**26.7**
Evangelical	285,480,000	4.1	13.1

Source: Center for the Study of Global Christianity. Pentecostals and charismatics are mutually exclusive categories. They overlap, however, with the evangelical category, and the three categories should not be added together. Many Christians do not identify with any of these movements. Population estimates are rounded to the ten thousands. Percentages are calculated from unrounded numbers. Pentecostal and charismatic figures may not add exactly due to rounding.

Pew Research Center's Forum on Religion & Public Life Global Christianity, December 2011

Figure 8. Christians by Movement[5]

Pentecostals by Region

Regions	PERCENTAGE OF REGION THAT IS PENTECOSTAL	PERCENTAGE OF WORLD PENTECOSTAL POPULATION
Americas	10.9%	36.7%
Sub-Saharan Africa	14.8	43.7
Asia-Pacific	1.1	15.5
Europe	1.5	4.0
Middle East-North Africa	0.1	0.1
World Total	**4.0**	**100.0**

Source: Pew Forum analysis of data from the Center for the Study of Global Christianity. Percentages may not add exactly due to rounding.

Pew Research Center's Forum on Religion & Public Life Global Christianity, December 2011

Charismatics by Region

Regions	PERCENTAGE OF REGION THAT IS CHARISMATICS	PERCENTAGE OF WORLD CHARISMATICS POPULATION
Americas	15.8%	48.5%
Sub-Saharan Africa	6.5	17.4
Asia-Pacific	2.2	29.5
Europe	1.8	4.3
Middle East-North Africa	0.2	0.3
World Total	**4.4**	**100.0**

Source: Pew Forum analysis of data from the Center for the Study of Global Christianity. Percentages may not add exactly due to rounding.

Pew Research Center's Forum on Religion & Public Life Global Christianity, December 2011

Figure 9. Pentecostals and Charismatics by Region[6]

While I was in Cape Town, South Africa, for Jakes Divinity School academic studies and advancement, the application of *sankofa* was in full effect. Sankofa is often associated with the proverb, "*Se wo were fi na wosankofa a yenkyi*," which translates as: "It is not wrong to go back for that which you have forgotten."[7] Using the sankofa framework to return to African roots enables church leadership to provide strategies for enhancing clergy understanding of IPV by offering historical, contemporary, and prospective perspectives.

---

5. Pew Research Center, "The New Face of Global Christianity."
6. Pew Research Center, "The New Face of Global Christianity."
7. Felder, "The Philosophical Approach of Sankofa."

An Alternative Solution for Institutional Pentecostalism

In an African feminist pragmatic cultural approach, emancipatory transformation is a proposed solution to address the issue of institutional Pentecostalism based in patriarchy, a risk factor promoting IPV and violence against women. This proposed solution aims to address the need for ethical leadership within Pentecostalism, since its patriarchal structure makes it susceptible to encouraging IPV and violence against women.

Two concepts govern the regulation of ethical leadership: responsibility and responsiveness. An ethical leader demonstrates high responsiveness to followers' needs, concerns, and interests, fostering collective progress toward shared objectives that yield advantages for the group members and the leader. An ethical leader assumes responsibility for the group of individuals under their leadership by embodying the qualities of a responsible steward. The characteristics of an ethical leader include acting with integrity and fulfilling the duties of caring for, protecting, guiding, organizing, serving, and sharing with their followers.[8] Ethical leaders possess a comprehensive understanding of their responsibilities, which entails adopting the position of servant leaders who prioritize their followers' well-being concerning the economy, ecology, and ecumenism.[9] Moreover, an ethical leader is purposeful and encompasses the following five principles: reverence for others' autonomy; dedication to serving others selflessly; commitment to justice, encompassing diversity, equity, and inclusion; adhering to honesty by being open and transparent; and fostering a sense of community by setting an example for their followers.[10] Ethical leaders' guiding principle is to prioritize avoiding causing harm. Hence, ethical leaders and their adherents should exhibit cultural sensitivity to comprehend the repercussions of their actions regarding violence against women and how such actions might shape the prevailing cultural and social norms and institutions within their operational context.

An African feminist pragmatic cultural approach is specific to the African context and does not seek to incorporate a Western feminist evaluation. African feminist paradigms typically assume that theological and ethical contemplation is based on a dedication to justice and the pursuit

---

8. Stückelberger et al., eds., "Responsible Leadership," 3–12.
9. Stückelberger et al., eds., "Responsible Leadership."
10. Stückelberger et al., eds., "Responsible Leadership."

of "the fullness of life" (John 10:10) for all individuals, particularly those marginalized, excluded, or oppressed by political systems and leaders.[11]

Figure 10. Patriarchy

Rhetorical question: Is it plausible to contemplate the notion that Gen 3:15 not only served as a prophetic indication of the advent of the Messiah, Jesus Christ, but also of the enduring societal structures, such as patriarchy? Is it possible to make the argument that enmity can be used as a conceptual framework to understand patriarchy, specifically in its antagonistic treatment of women?

The African feminist pragmatic cultural approach adopts Rebecca Chopp's promotion of the theory of emancipatory transformation. This approach "recognizes that theological and ethical reflections are historically, individually, and socially contextual."[12] This leadership model assumes no universal "correct action" but allows each argument to develop constructively according to its specific context.[13] The approach facilitates the promotion of justice, the formation of policies and laws, support for

11. Stückelberger et al., eds., "Responsible Leadership."
12. Stückelbergeret al., eds., "Responsible Leadership."
13. Stückelberger et al., eds., "Responsible Leadership."

women's rights organizations, and the opportunity to challenge norms and attitudes that discriminate against women and girls, especially regarding the acceptability of violence against women. Therefore, this model provides the scaffolding to focus on social and attitude norms that foster violence against women. Despite its cultural context in Africa, its versatility allows for its use in diverse cultural settings around the globe. This leadership model gives women and girls a face and voice to be seen and heard in public spaces. It also ensures equality in leadership roles for women in the church, government, community, and communal family life.

The proposed alternative option is met with opposition from conventional fundamentalism and fundamentalists, as they do not endorse viewpoints advocating for social change or any programs promoting gender equality. In the examined context of fundamentalism, the non-denominational perspective acknowledges feminism and the feminist movement as potentially detrimental to both genders.[14] This perspective argues that the feminist movement, in its pursuit of empowering women to assert their autonomy and pursue independence, may diminish the traditional concept of masculinity among men and create a situation where women are left vulnerable due to the absence of the protective role traditionally associated with men.[15]

While traditionally dominant cultural narratives often framed men as breadwinners and women as homemakers, many women, especially African American women, long worked outside the home, often out of necessity, including in roles as domestic laborers and caregivers. Now, both women and men across ethnicities work. Some men are capable of financially taking care of their wives, but because feminism encourages this idea of career women, women have given up the care of their children to daycare centers and nannies. Feminism dismantles the headship and sets up a matriarchy. Feminism, they argue, goes against God's divine will.[16]

Even with this anti-feminist argument, Pentecostalism has the potential to be "gender sensitive" to serve as a platform for addressing global political concerns, such as the pervasive issue of violence against women and girls, as well as the need for enhanced global democratic participation. The prosperity gospel is a significant component of Pentecostalism and is frequently associated with its sermons and teachings. Therefore, one could

14. Soares, "Eden after Eve."
15. Soares, "Eden after Eve."
16. Soares, "Eden after Eve."

argue that the concepts of "class and gender" are central to Pentecostalism. This theological framework emphasizes the potential for spiritual blessings to facilitate upward social mobility, particularly for individuals experiencing poverty, and serves as a means to address gender-based inequalities, particularly for women.

As an illustration, African Pentecostalism has facilitated the inclusion of African women in leadership positions within the church and their respective communities. Teresia Wairimu, a Kenyan woman associated with the Faith Evangelistic Ministry, has garnered significant global recognition for her contributions to Kenya and other nations. Numerous female Pentecostal leaders, such as Wairimu, leverage soft power to launch social welfare programs, lead humanitarian efforts, build successful businesses, drive peacebuilding initiatives, promote national unity, and cultivate influential social networks.[17] Another example to further illustrate the egalitarian nature of women's leadership within African Pentecostalism in establishing and expanding Pentecostal churches in Botswana. African Pentecostalism has allowed women to operate in leadership roles equal to men, planting and growing Pentecostal churches in Botswana and thus changing the patriarchal religious terrain, considering that women in Botswana's culture are subordinate and marginalized. This development has transformed the patriarchal religious landscape, particularly in light of the prevailing cultural norms.[18]

An Alternative Solution for Pentecostal Hermeneutics

According to Elisabeth Schussler Fiorenza, limited awareness regarding women depicted in religious texts can be attributed, in part, to the androcentric nature of religious teachings and liturgical practices, which have significantly influenced the Christian collective imagination.[19] Androcentrism is the ideology or practice of placing males at the center of how one views the world and its culture and history, yielding a masculine point of view, a patriarchal ethos.[20] Fiorenza presents a theoretical framework for the implementation of a feminist biblical interpretation. This approach centers

17. Seleina Parsitau, "Soft Tongue, Powerful Voice, Huge Influence," 159–80.
18. Nkomazana, "The Role of Women, Theology, and Ecumenical Organizations," 181–202.
19. Schussler Fiorenza, *But She Said*, 22.
20. Schussler Fiorenza, *But She Said*, 23.

on the androcentric characteristics of biblical texts and explores alternative approaches to their translation that are deemed less androcentric. A feminist approach to biblical interpretation seeks to address and rectify gender inequalities within the biblical text while critically reevaluating traditional interpretations.[21] This framework focuses on examining individual identity and utilizing biblical imagination.[22] It aims to highlight women's voices by recovering works of intellectual writing by women.[23] This paradigm centers its attention on examining women in the Bible from a historical perspective while also proposing a reevaluation of the objectives of early Christian historiography.[24] It also focuses on the ideological representations in texts that prioritize male perspectives and redirects attention toward women as active readers.[25] Finally, the framework acknowledges the sociopolitical, global-cultural, and diversified religious backgrounds and circumstances in which biblical reading occurs.[26]

Maria Clara Bingermer commented on Gen 1:26, "Throughout biblical tradition in the economy of the covenant, that which is divine (God, Jesus, and Christ) is represented with masculine elements and that which is human (Israel, the church) with feminine elements. Androcentrism and theocentrism are parallel . . . [T]he male gender symbolizes the excellence of the divine image."[27]

Fundamentalism and fundamentalist theology generally do not endorse a feminist perspective in their interpretation of the Scriptures. Their argument is rooted in their understanding of an androcentric God and the hierarchical nature of the relationship between men and women, as derived from their interpretation of Gen 1 and 2. Fundamentalists strongly believe in the infallibility of the Bible and advocate for a literal approach to interpreting its contents. "It is this belief that the Bible is an unquestionable authority that does not require interpretation that has implications for women and their role and status in the family, marriage, and church ministry and, indeed, society."[28]

21. Schussler Fiorenza, *But She Said*, 23.
22. Schussler Fiorenza, *But She Said*, 26.
23. Schussler Fiorenza, *But She Said*, 28.
24. Schussler Fiorenza, *But She Said*, 30–31.
25. Schussler Fiorenza, *But She Said*, 34–35.
26. Schussler Fiorenza, *But She Said*, 37.
27. Bingemer, "Reflections on the Trinity," quoted in Soares, "Eden after Eve."
28. Soares, "Eden after Eve."

The fundamentalists' adherence to a literal interpretation of the Bible may be deemed flawed, rendering them susceptible to critique and indicating the necessity for an alternate viewpoint. Based on Gen 1:27 and Gal 3:28, it is asserted that God fashioned both the male and female genders in his image, emphasizing the equality and unity of all individuals in Christ. The concept highlights the egalitarianism and solidarity of all individuals within their association with Christ. These Bible verses suggest an inherent equality between men and women from a divine standpoint, thereby indicating the need for equitable treatment between the two genders.

In her 2019 study titled "Spiritual Justice: Toward a Womanish Spirituality of Spiritual Care," Sonia Hinds presents a hermeneutical framework that integrates spiritual care and spiritual justice for girls and women survivors who have experienced sexual acts of violence and rape. Spiritual justice requires reexamining girls' and women's historical and religious contexts and permitting a sympathetic and social justice approach, as Jesus Christ showed in the canonical Gospels with the woman "caught" in adultery.[29] Spiritual care restores the whole person—physical, psychological, and spiritual—instead of diagnosing and treating women as just flesh.[30]

This framework offers a distinct perspective from the ideologies of fundamentalism. Hinds' study employs a qualitative approach and utilizes the hermeneutic phenomenological framework developed by Susanne Laverty.[31] The primary objective of this framework is to analyze the human experience within a particular context. The analysis was carried out in Barbados, suggesting the potential applicability of this approach in many geographical contexts due to Barbados' key role in the historical development of the African diaspora.

---

29. Hinds, "Spiritual Justice," 293, 298–99.
30. Hinds, "Spiritual Justice," 299.
31. Hinds, "Spiritual Justice," 292.

Recognize

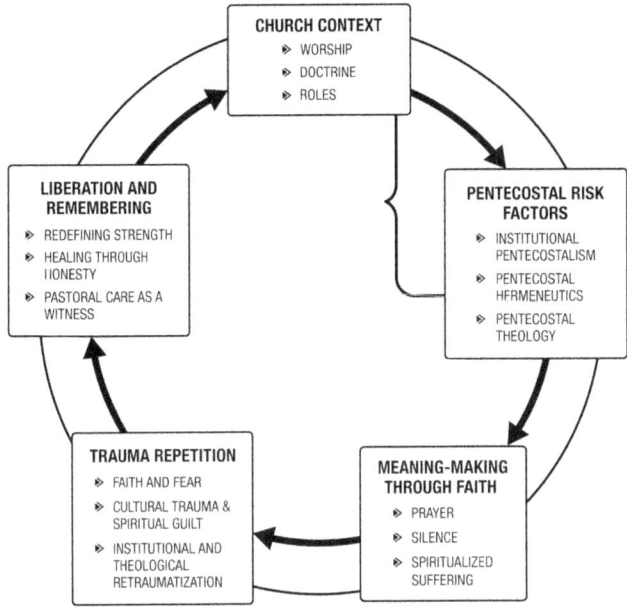

Figure 11. A Hermeneutic Phenomenology of African American Women's Lived Experiences with IPV in Pentecostal Ministry

This hermeneutic phenomenology infographic was shaped by the lived stories of African American women who have survived intimate partner violence within Pentecostal ministry contexts and who participated in focus groups. Their voices, too often silenced or overlooked, have profoundly informed this work. Here, you see a high-level representation of their journeys, offering a window into the spiritual, emotional, and communal realities they navigate. It is both a witness and a call to listen, understand, and respond with compassionate, theologically grounded care.

Hinds's conceptualization of "womanish theology and spirituality" advocates for recognizing and applying "gender-sensitive" methodologies when engaging with Scriptures and liturgy. Specifically, it seeks to explore the influence of traumatic experiences on their theological viewpoints, particularly concerning their inquiries about the role of God and the church in their recovery journey. Theological questions survivors may have include:

Where was God when all this was happening to me? What would my Sunday school/priest/pastor say if I told her/him? Would she or he even believe me? Is she/he able to help me? Can my male pastor help me? Because of this, will I go to hell? If the Bible tells me to honor and obey my parents, how could this happen to me? Am I a bad person, and so God let this happen to me?[32]

Hinds emphasizes establishing secure and non-judgmental environments inside the church to support female survivors. However, the task of establishing such a milieu presents significant difficulties. The Anglican Church holds the distinction of being the first Christian religious institution established in Barbados. Hinds posits that the Anglican Church's lack of gender awareness is a matter of great importance, primarily stemming from the pervasive use of masculine imagery in its liturgy and ceremonies. Female survivors may encounter masculine iconography, potentially impacting their spiritual healing journey. Hinds provides an illustrative instance of her apprehension within the Gloria in Excelsis, a liturgical prayer chanted during each Eucharistic ceremony.

> Glory to God in the highest,
> and peace to his people on earth.
> Lord God, heavenly King,
> Almighty God and Father,
> we worship you, we give you thanks,
> we praise you for your glory.
> Lord God, Lamb of God,
> you take away the sin of the World:
> have mercy on us;
> you are seated at the right hand of the Father:
> receive our prayer.
> For you alone are the Holy One,
> you alone are the Lord,
> you alone are the Most High,
> Jesus Christ, with the Holy Spirit,
> in the glory of God the Father, Amen[33]

The words "king," "father," "Lord," "son," and "his" all have solid male meanings. According to Hinds, language impacts our cognitive processes and interpretations. Unsurprisingly, a woman who has experienced abuse may struggle to perceive her body as her own following the traumatic event and may even encounter challenges in reciting the prayer "Our Father" as she previously did.[34] Consequently, for women to achieve a sense of

---

32. Hinds, "Spiritual Justice," 299.
33. Hinds, "Spiritual Justice," 305–6.
34. Hinds, "Spiritual Justice."

completeness, it is imperative to employ inclusive language that incorporates their unique realities and experiences into liturgical practices.[35]

Hinds suggests the application of biblical assurance, as advised by Cooper-White, as a therapeutic strategy that can be beneficial in the recovery process of survivors. It is important to note that imposing scriptures on a survivor should be avoided, and instead, they should be supplied upon the survivor's request.[36] Adopting a literal and concrete approach to the scriptures may be less effective in facilitating healing.[37] Statements of assurance, such as "God keeps you safe," may not necessarily align with a survivor's literal, tangible reality. She may see this statement as being dishonest and retraumatizing.[38]

The alternative solutions put forth by Fiorenza and Hinds are deliberately chosen to initiate discussions regarding a patriarchal lens through which Christendom approached hermeneutical interpretation of Scripture, the use of iconography in Scripture and liturgy, and the application of Scriptures in supporting women who have experienced violence and sexual abuse. When these measures are considered, they may reduce the IPV risk factors associated with Pentecostal hermeneutics.

An Alternative Solution to Pentecostal Trinity Theology

Pentecostal Trinity theology plays a foundational role in the institution of Pentecostalism and in Pentecostal hermeneutics; consequently, when the Trinity is viewed as a patriarchal, hierarchical structure, it can be inferred that this theological perspective contributes to the ongoing risk factors that may prevent clergy from being able to advocate effectively for women who are victim-survivors of IPV. The theological framework of Pentecostal trinity theology, which incorporates the divine entities of God the Father, God the Son, and God the Holy Spirit, is not disputed. Instead, it is the application of a hierarchical structure to the arrangement of individuals, specifically men, women, and children, with males assuming a superior position as the leaders of homes. Implementing this paradigm forms a male-centered viewpoint throughout all three ministry techniques within the

---

35. Hinds, "Spiritual Justice," 306.
36. Hinds, "Spiritual Justice," 308.
37. Hinds, "Spiritual Justice," 308.
38. Cooper-White, *Violence Against Women*, quoted in Sonia Hinds, "Spiritual Justice," 308.

Pentecostal tradition. The debate arises as to how one may attain the necessary equilibrium to guarantee gender equality and inclusivity throughout all levels of Pentecostalism. Let's examine a case study on the Apostolic Teaching Center (ATC), a prototype women-centered ministry. This study showcases its potential for advancing equality in human relationships by eliminating the patriarchal hierarchy within Pentecostalism.

Pastor Eliseus Joseph and co-pastor Marcia Joseph founded the ATC in Barbados. The ministry might be characterized as a "gender egalitarian" ministry since it seeks to challenge the prevailing ideology and practice of patriarchy, which entails male domination and the subjection of women through specific misinterpretations of biblical texts.[39] The primary objective of the ATC is to establish a ministry that is centered on women and attentive to gender-related concerns, achieved through a process of reinterpreting Scripture.[40] The foundation of the ministry is established upon prayer and the dispensation of grace. This framework advocates for including women in all levels of society, church leadership, and ministry, asserting their right to have a voice and participate actively.

The ATC adopts an interpretive stance toward reexamining Scripture, drawing primarily from the texts found in Gen chapters 1 and 2. Pastor Joseph argues that the initial two chapters of Genesis do not exhibit a patriarchal framework or endorse a hierarchical arrangement.[41] Furthermore, he asserts that God never intended such a system. Joseph proceeds to argue against the claim that the Bible is patriarchal. He highlights that patriarchy is a societal construct rather than a biblical one.[42] Hence, Pastor Joseph claims that the patriarchal nature of the church can be attributed to the theological concept of sin, as exemplified in the narrative of the fall of humanity.[43] The interpretation of Eve's curse as a justification for male dominance is situated within the framework of patriarchy. Eve's curse could potentially be interpreted as a strategy employed by the church to validate the dominance of males and reinforce the notion of women's inferiority, thereby upholding the existing social order in ministry and society.[44] The perspective of ATC acknowledges that both men and women, who are

---

39. Soares, "Eden after Eve."
40. Soares, "Eden after Eve."
41. Soares, "Eden after Eve."
42. Soares, "Eden after Eve."
43. Soares, "Eden after Eve."
44. Soares, "Eden after Eve."

created in the image and likeness of God, are inherently equal (Gen 1:27). The ministry places a primary emphasis on the Kingdom of God (Gal 3:28, Joel 2:28), recognizing that the church often adopts a narrow perspective that is incongruent with the Kingdom of God. Consequently, the ministry adopts a more comprehensive approach to include models of women from the Old and New Testament, the models of faith, authority, and power.

Besancon Spencer provides a summary:

> Junia is called an apostle, Mary Magdalene, Joanna, Mary mother of Jesus, Mary mother of James and Salome mother of James and John were "apostle." Anna, a prophet, as were Miriam, Huldah, the wife of Isaiah, and Deborah, Phillip's four daughters, prophesied as did the women at Corinth. Priscilla and the women at Crete were teachers. The women at Crete were elderly. Priscilla, as well as a coworker and church overseer.[45]

The Kingdom of God is a comprehensive perspective on God's sovereignty, encompassing various aspects such as political governance, social dynamics, economic systems, and cultural influences. It aims to establish a society that upholds principles of justice and dignity for all individuals, as referenced in John 10:10.[46] The leadership of ATC also calls for the reinterpretation of the word submission in Eph 5:22. "The ministry's official stance is that the act of submission within a marital relationship is considered mutual and limited to the husband and wife."[47] The reinterpretation challenges conventional notions that advocate for women's submission to men in familial, occupational, and religious contexts.[48]

> Wives, submit yourselves to your own husbands as you do to the Lord. For the husband is the head of the wife as Christ is the head of the church, his body, of which he is the Savior. Now, as the church submits to Christ, so also wives should submit to their husbands in everything (Eph 5:22–24).

A feminist complementary reinterpretation of men and women in Eph 5:22–24 may provide an intervention for IPV and heighten the awareness of IPV and gender violence worldwide. A complementary illustration of Eph 5:22–24:

---

45. Spencer, *Beyond the Cruse*, quoted in Soares, "Eden after Eve."
46. Soares, "Eden after Eve."
47. Soares, "Eden after Eve."
48. Soares, "Eden after Eve."

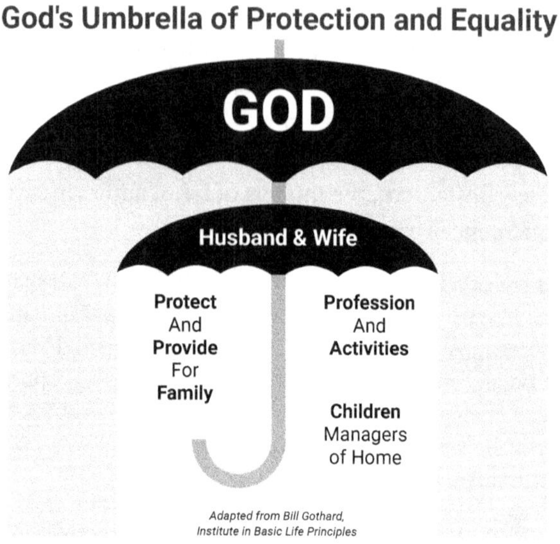

God's Umbrella of Protection and Equality

Figure 12. God's Umbrella of Protection (Complementary)

ATC acknowledges that feminism and the feminist movement possess both positive and negative attributes. The ATC perspective posits that feminism aims to redefine the concept of women, address gender imbalances, challenge male dominance, and advocate for gender-specific demands in pursuit of equality, justice, and social progress.[49] This movement seeks to bring about transformative changes in society and promote fairness. Nevertheless, the ministry acknowledges the potential drawbacks associated with feminism and the feminist movement, as it can inadvertently contribute to a social construct that fails to recognize men as equal social counterparts.[50]

Conclusion

I explored different ways the Pentecostal community can help reduce the risk of IPV. Pentecostalism exhibits ambivalence toward women and may actively encourage the mistreatment of women and children within the church, household, and community. Any solution to the institutional problems within Pentecostalism, including its hermeneutics and theology, must include women in church leadership, including priestly positions like

---

49. Soares, "Eden after Eve."
50. Soares, "Eden after Eve."

elders, pastors, and bishops, to ensure gender equality and give women a voice. Bishop Gwendolyn Weeks, Senior Pastor of Bethel Tabernacle Pentecostal Church in Boston, Massachusetts, became the first woman to join the Bishops' Council for the Pentecostal Assemblies of the World in 2022, marking a significant milestone in the organization's century-long history.[51] However, this case illustrates the Pentecostal world's lag in integrating women into ministerial roles. To promote gender equality, biblical interpretation may require adopting gender-sensitive solutions. Church leaders must actively identify barriers to IPV education, particularly those rooted in androcentric male dominance. While the alternative solutions propose strategies for addressing patriarchal systems within the church, they do not offer an optimal approach for raising awareness about IPV and reducing the specific risk factors that prevent clergy from understanding, acknowledging, responding to, and preventing the retraumatization of women who are survivors of IPV within Pentecostal communities.

However, a transformative path unfolds before us that leads to embracing trauma-informed theology. This journey is a vital step in reshaping the church's response to IPV. It's not just a new method, but a faithful return to the heart of pastoral care. In Ezekiel 34, God rebukes the shepherds of Israel for failing to tend the flock, saying, "You have not strengthened the weak or healed the sick or bound up the injured . . . so they were scattered because there was no shepherd." Trauma-informed theology invites us to become the kind of shepherds God calls for—those who notice the wounded, protect the vulnerable, and restore the scattered.

In John 10:14, Jesus declares, "I am the good shepherd. I know my sheep and my sheep know me." That intimacy and attentiveness are what trauma-informed pastoral care strives to embody: to see, to know, and to care with compassion and clarity.

The next chapter will delve into why trauma-informed theology powerfully aligns with our pastoral calling. Genuine pastoral care does not turn away from suffering. It moves toward it, just as Christ did when he proclaimed in Luke 4:18, "The Spirit of the Lord is upon me . . . He has sent me to bind up the brokenhearted, to proclaim liberty to the captives." Trauma-informed ministry reflects this mission. It brings light to hidden places, opens space for truth, and offers hope. Hope for healing. Hope for justice. And hope that the church might finally become the sanctuary it was always meant to be in word, presence, and power.

---

51. Bethlehem Apostolic Church, "Pentecostal Assemblies of the World."

3

Respond

Dear clergy colleagues,

As we step into this next chapter together, I invite you to pause with me. We are not just ministers of the Gospel but also shepherds, listeners, and guides who have walked alongside others in their deepest pain. Your role is significant, and your presence is powerful in this sacred task.

From the very beginning of the Bible, we catch glimpses of trauma. Take a few moments to reflect on Gen 1:1–2. The earth was *formless and void*, cloaked in darkness, and the Spirit of God hovered over the deep. Have you ever wondered what preceded that moment of divine movement? What kind of chaos or rupture made the world so empty that it required the full creative force of God to bring it into order? There is something there—something unspoken—that hints at disruption, disorder ... trauma.

And then, in Gen 3:15, right after the fall, we receive the first whisper of the Gospel, a messianic promise that speaks not just to sin but to suffering: "He will crush your head, and you will strike his heel." Embedded in this prophecy is the reality of violence, pain, and sacrifice. Yet, it's also the seed of hope. A Savior would come, one who would feel the full weight of humanity's trauma and still choose to redeem it.

Let's consider a transformative perspective: What if trauma isn't just a peripheral aspect of our theology but a central one? What if trauma-informed theology isn't a passing trend but a return to the core of our faith? A truth we've always known: God sees, hears, and responds to suffering. This realization can inspire renewed hope and a deeper understanding of God's love and grace.

Using the trauma-informed care model—the 4Rs: realize, recognize, respond, and resist retraumatization—we can understand how the Gospel has always been trauma-informed:

- **Realize:** Humanity fell. God saw the need for redemption.

  Gen 3, Rom 5:12, John 3:16

- **Recognize:** God, in his holiness, acknowledged that no human could be blameless without divine intervention.

  Ps 14:2-3, Ps 51:5, 1 John 3:8

- **Respond:** God wrapped himself in flesh, sent Jesus, and, through his death and resurrection, made healing possible.

  Eph 1:7, Rom 6:9, 1 Cor 15:20

- **Resist Retraumatization:** Jesus promised the Holy Spirit—the Comforter, Advocate, and Healer—who lives within us and strengthens us to heal and help others heal.

  John 14:16-18, Rom 8:26-27, Gal 5:22-23

As we journey through the pages ahead, remember that this exploration is not a departure from sound doctrine but a deepening of it. It's a fuller expression of pastoral care, a call for us, as Pentecostal clergy, to minister with a renewed sense of presence and power. This is not just a call; it's an inspiration and motivation for us to minister with a renewed sense of presence and power.

Let's enter this sacred conversation together with open hearts, Bibles, and ears tuned to the Spirit.

Introduction

Trauma can be described as a distressing occurrence or incident that may be caused by human actions such as IPV, sexual assault, warfare, or industrial accidents, or by natural events like earthquakes or tornadoes.[1] Anita Phillips defines trauma as "anything that changes your perspective on yourself, other people, the world, or God, and when your perspective on God

---

1. APA Dictionary of Psychology, s.v. "Trauma."

has changed, that is spiritual trauma."[2] The impact of adverse traumatic experiences on an individual's worldview and religious beliefs might result in a perception of the world as hostile and lacking in safety. This perception can lead to intense emotional states, including but not limited to anxiety, helplessness, dissociation, disorientation, and other disruptive affective experiences, which can significantly impair individuals' general well-being and interpersonal connections.

Collective trauma refers to a catastrophic occurrence that profoundly disrupts the fundamental fabric of a society. COVID-19 resulted in a worldwide collective trauma in 2020, and its ripple effects will be experienced for generations to come. COVID-19 is a contagious illness caused by a virus that affects the lungs and can spread quickly from person to person. It first appeared in late 2019 and changed daily life worldwide, impacting our health, communities, and connections. The Kaiser Family Foundation conducted data analysis of surveys comparing data points from 2019 to 2021 and reported the following percentages of people with anxiety and depression in the US due to COVID-19–related stressors:[3]

- 56 percent of young adults (ages 18–24)
- 48 percent of Black adults
- 46 percent of Hispanic or Latino adults
- 41 percent of white adults

It is imperative to note that 13 percent of adults from the survey reported new or increased substance use, and 11 percent of adults had suicidal ideation.[4] Stressors experienced included job loss, financial uncertainty, isolation, death, grief, suffering, the fear of contracting the virus, and a lack of psychosocial system support.

IPV drastically intensified both nationally and globally at the onset of COVID-19 in 2020. During the COVID-19 lockdowns, domestic violence reports surged globally, rising by 22 to 300 percent depending on the region.[5] Stay-at-home orders may have put those at risk for IPV in greater danger. Most churches closed their doors—92 percent of Evangelicals, 94 percent of Catholics, 96 percent of mainline Protestants, and 79 percent

---

2. Phillips, "A Spiritual Approach to Trauma Recovery."
3. Panchal, et al., "The Implications of COVID-19."
4. Panchal, et al., "The Implications of COVID-19."
5. Boserup, et al., "Alarming Trends," 2753–55.

of historically Black churches. While many shifted to online services, vital support systems like women's and children's ministries—often lifelines for resilience—were suddenly out of reach during one of the most difficult times in a generation.[6] The collective grief, uncertainty, and isolation we've endured through the COVID-19 pandemic pulled back the curtain on just how severely trauma touches every part of our lives: body, mind, spirit, and community. For many, the church became a lifeline; for others, it was a place where pain went unspoken or unacknowledged. This moment has made it undeniable: we can no longer afford to minister without a framework that honors the wounds people carry. Trauma-informed theology meets us right there in the thick of it with the promise that healing is not just possible but sacred. As Isaiah reminds us, *"by his stripes, we are healed."* That healing is not abstract; it requires us to show up differently, more aware, more compassionate, and more Spirit-led in how we serve.

Trauma-Informed Theology

Biblical Foundation

Serving God's people requires advocating for theology that considers trauma. The historical context of Christian theology is marked by the presence of trauma, which influences our efforts to interpret the Bible's teachings on God, salvation, and our purpose in the world. In biblical times, there was no conceptual framework to define trauma. Nevertheless, the language of trauma permeates the Scriptures. In examining the language employed by David in Ps 55:1–6, it becomes apparent that he depicts four distinct stress responses commonly observed in individuals who have experienced trauma. These stress responses include flight, fight, freeze, and fawn, each used as a coping mechanism to evade conflict.

> Listen to my prayer, O God, do not ignore my plea; hear me and answer me. My thoughts trouble me, and I am distraught because of what my enemy is saying, because of the threats of the wicked, for they bring down suffering on me and assail me in their anger. My heart is in anguish within me; the terrors of death have fallen on me. Fear and trembling have beset me; horror has overwhelmed me. I said, "Oh, that I had the wings of a dove! I would fly away and be at rest. I would flee far away and stay in the desert."[7]

---

6. Gecewicz, "Few Americans Say Their House of Worship is Open."
7. Ps 55:1–6 (NIV).

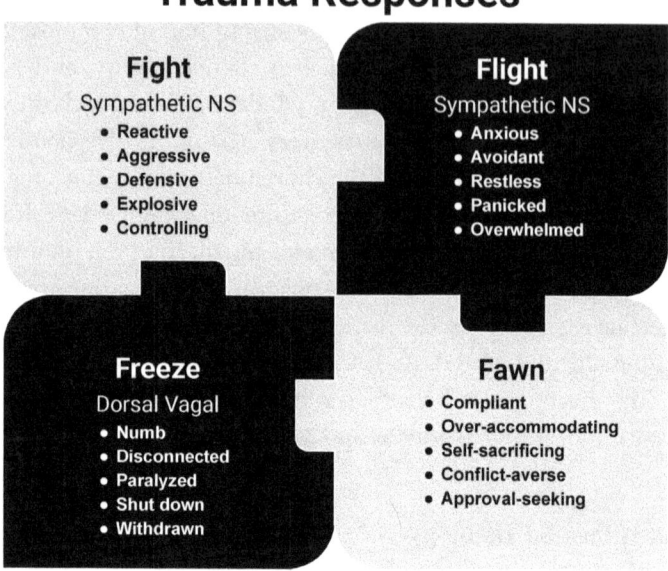

Figure 13. The Four Fs of Trauma Response: Fight, Flight, Freeze, Fawn

Nadine Burke Harris, a medical physician, informs that when encountering a traumatic event, our brain sends neurotransmitter signals to the amygdala, the brain's fear center.[8] The amygdala transmits signals to the adrenal glands, stimulating the synthesis of stress-inducing substances, including adrenaline and cortisol. As a result, the individual experiences a heightened heart rate, widened pupils, and rapid breathing, which then triggers one of the four trauma responses. David likely experienced these same physiological reactions to stress and didn't hide it; he wrote about his anguish in the Psalms.

Trauma Theology

In the late twentieth century, the discipline of psychology concentrated on a body of studies known as "trauma theory," which examined the effects of various traumatic experiences, including assault, rape, war, famine, and imprisonment, on individuals, resulting in the official acknowledgment of

---

8. Burke Harris, *The Deepest Well*, 48–49.

post-traumatic stress disorder (PTSD) in the 1980s.[9] The issue with PTSD is its tendency to become deeply ingrained; the stress reaction gets fixated on prior events, continuously repeating itself.[10] Individuals with PTSD experience a recurring stress response that frequently confuses present stimuli with past events to such an extent that it becomes challenging for the survivor to function in the present moment effectively.[11]

Having a clear understanding of PTSD is imperative. Women are more likely to develop PTSD than men; 8 percent of women and 4 percent of men will develop the disorder.[12,13] O'Doherty says people with PTSD are more likely to experience violence in personal and social relationships.[14] IPV puts women at greater risk of developing PTSD. Some symptoms of PTSD are increased arousal, high levels of vigilance, hearing and looking for danger, an exaggerated startle response, outbursts of anger, and consistently being in fight-or-flight mode. It is also important to note that 70 percent of adults in the US reported experiencing some traumatic event in their lifetime.[15] Additionally, 20 percent of people diagnosed with PTSD will develop another diagnosis, such as depression or anxiety.[16] Clergy need to be able to respond to congregants when a mental health emergency or challenge arises in the congregation.

Trauma theology precepts are extracted from trauma theory, which has expanded since the 1990s into an interdisciplinary field that extends beyond psychology to encompass literature, history, and philosophy, focusing on exploring topics related to memory, forgetting, and storytelling.[17] Trauma theology aims to take biblical text and analyze it through the hermeneutic lens of trauma. Analyzing the hermeneutics of trauma language presented in the Bible using trauma theology offers a valuable framework to understanding the human journey toward healing from trauma and gaining insight into God. Trauma hermeneutics provides additional ways for studying potentially traumatic events and their aftermath seamlessly incorporated in biblical texts' social and cultural contexts, including where

9. Oxford Reference, "Trauma Theory."
10. Burke Harris, *The Deepest Well*, 47.
11. Burke Harris, *The Deepest Well*, 47.
12. Vernor, "PTSD is More Likely in Women Than Men."
13. National Center for PTSD, "How Common is PTSD in Adults?"
14. O'Doherty, "Introduction to PTSD."
15. O'Doherty, "Introduction to PTSD."
16. The Recovery Village, "PTSD Statistics and Facts."
17. Oxford Reference, "Trauma Theory."

the Bible is received and used and where it can traumatize readers. "Trauma hermeneutics allows us to read Scripture, especially the stories of biblical characters, through the lens of the four Rs, helping us care more compassionately for those experiencing trauma today."[18]

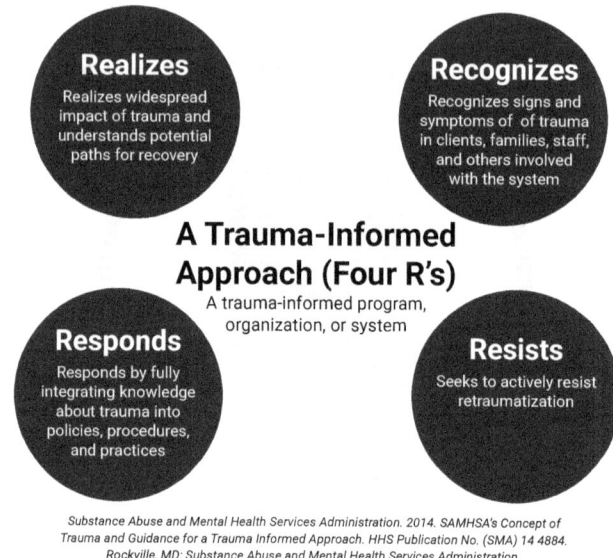

Substance Abuse and Mental Health Services Administration. 2014. SAMHSA's Concept of Trauma and Guidance for a Trauma Informed Approach. HHS Publication No. (SMA) 14 4884. Rockville, MD: Substance Abuse and Mental Health Services Administration.

Figure 14. A Trauma-Informed Approach (Four Rs)[19]

Trauma-informed care is a methodical strategy that helps service providers and organizations realize the prevalence of trauma, while creating an environment that promotes healing and recovery from trauma. There are six guiding principles of a trauma-informed approach:[20]

1. Safety
2. Trustworthiness and transparency
3. Peer support
4. Collaboration and mutuality
5. Empowerment, voice, and choice
6. Cultural, historical, and gender issues

18. McDonald, "Hermeneutics of Trauma and the Bible."
19. Substance Abuse and Mental Health Services Administration, SAMHSA's Concept of Trauma and Guidance for a Trauma-Informed Approach.
20. Wilson, et al., "Trauma-Informed Care."

Trauma theology is essential to Christian theology, yet there is a noticeable gap in qualitative research that explores how trauma-informed care can be practically integrated into the life and structure of the church. This work seeks to help fill that gap.

Pedagogy of Trauma-Informed Theology

Trauma-informed theology enables the minister to observe the survivor expressing grief and sorrow over the losses experienced in overcoming trauma while also providing an opportunity to witness the manifestation of God's magnificence, existence, and influence in the aftermath of violence.[21] Trauma-informed theology enables the minister to bear witness from a position between the experiences of trauma and grace. According to Alex R. Wendel, trauma-informed theology helps religious leaders remain rooted in their understanding of God and make sense of God's nature, presence, and purpose in the midst of human suffering. Because of this framework, "theologians are better able to (1) maintain a high view of God and Christian doctrine and (2) affirm and meet the needs of traumatized individuals with the therapeutic resources of the Christian faith."[22]

Trauma-informed theology understands that the hallmark of the trauma-informed care principle is not to harm. It incorporates the guiding principles of trauma-informed care into all aspects of ministry programming and liturgy. This doctrine considers the impact of trauma along the continuum of life that encompasses the intersectionality of age, gender, social, culture, marital status, and sexual orientation. Jennifer Baldwin suggests four elements when constructing trauma-informed theology: "the priority of the bodily experience, acceptance of trauma narratives, natural given-ness of human psychological multiplicity, and religious praxis is robust faith in human resiliency."[23]

I interviewed Joni S. Sancken, a trauma-informed theologian, and asked her to define trauma-informed theology. She explained:

> What is trauma-informed theology? I think it's that sense of allowing that experience, that human experience, to be factored into how we understand who God is toward us and how we understand

---

21. Travis, *Unspeakable*, new studies in theology and trauma, Location 111. Kindle.
22. Wendel, "Trauma-Informed Theology or Theologically Informed Trauma?" 3–26.
23. Baldwin, *Trauma-Sensitive Theology*, 7–9.

what it is to be human. So, it's a little feminist theology, womanist theology, liberation theology. It's allowing a particular aspect of human experience to have a say in our theological system that we're constructing.[24]

Additionally, I had the privilege of interviewing Sarah Travis, a trauma-informed theologian, and asked her the following question, "Do you feel, from your experience and in general, that the church is creating spaces for us to have that dialogue about trauma, whether it is coming from the pulpit or within the ministry?"

> I think, in general, people's awareness of trauma has increased in recent years. I think it has finally hit the realm of Christian theology. Sometimes, things take a lot longer to get to Christian theology than they should, especially since the trauma is so much at the core of everything that's in scripture; it's at the core of the Christian experience. And I think around the pandemic, there's been greater conversation about trauma. But I don't think for a second that we pay enough attention. I mean, the awareness is simply not there that these events that happen in our world are traumatizing us in the pews; at least, I'm talking about white, affluent congregations that don't get that trauma is also about them.[25]

I also spoke with Chris Haughee, who has deep expertise in trauma-informed ministry:

> When I see those connections between trauma-informed principles and scripture, it's not something that threatens my faith. It's something that bolsters my faith. [. . .] It's more than the approach to scripture, just like in trauma, and this is where I love this space that I'm in as a minister because I see trauma-informed ministry as it's not a program. It's not a teaching series or something we take our church through. It's a lens by which we view our lives and we view our scripture and the connection between the two.[26]

Trauma-informed theology connects the pulpit with the trauma in the pews. However, it may be underutilized because both the church and broader society often operate within systemic patriarchal structures that hinder its influence on leadership. Gert J. Malan reminds us that "in patriarchal societies, the principal symbolizations of all social relations are in

---

24. Joni S. Sancken, interviewed by Bridget P. Robinson, November 21, 2022.
25. Sarah Travis, interviewed by Bridget P. Robinson, November 10, 2022.
26. Chris Haughee, interviewed by Bridget P. Robinson, November 10, 2022

terms of the father's kinship role as head of the family, where women and children are treated as property."[27] Senior leadership roles in the church are overwhelmingly filled by men, who may oppose trauma-informed theology. There is a possibility that a male abuser may have a leadership position, which might lead to opposition toward trauma-informed theology. There may be a perceived shift in power and control if increased awareness of IPV is achieved among the clergy.

Groome asserts that pedagogy incorporating trauma-informed theology empowers pastors to act as catalysts for change, informing and transforming individuals' essence within society.[28] Both trauma and pedagogy exert influence on individuals' theological beliefs, their perception of self, and their ability to take action within communities that promote gender equality.

Methods and Methodology

I knew that listening deeply to lived experiences would be the most faithful and effective way to understand the real impact of trauma and IPV in the lives of Black women of faith. When approaching my dissertation, I chose a qualitative approach, utilizing focus groups and interviews, because I wanted to create a sacred space for voices that are often overlooked or silenced. I leaned on Astley's wisdom, understanding that ordinary theology lives in everyday language, in the stories people tell, and even in what goes unsaid.[29] My role was to listen with care, to discern both the spoken and unspoken truths that emerged from those sacred conversations. Because the women I spoke with shared personal and often painful stories, it was essential to ensure their safety and dignity. That's why I sought and received ethical approval from the George Fox University Institutional Review Board (IRB) so the study could be carried out with integrity, accountability, and deep respect for each participant's humanity.

I facilitated two focus groups and nine informal interviews, all of which provided real-life examples in a ministry context of how IPV is a problem that disproportionately affects African American women. The study participants included African American women living in urban U.S. cities, IPV survivors, Christian mental health professionals, domestic

27. Malan, "God's Patronage."
28. Groome, *Sharing Faith*, 8.
29. Astley, *Ordinary Theology*, 121.

violence advocates, and women who serve as ministry leaders across various areas of the church.

Focus Group and Interview Analysis

Overall, the study participants believe that the church awareness of IPV has increased over the years; however, the participants characterized this awareness as passive. As co-pastor of her church, Dr. Susie C. Owens, notes:

> Years ago, there was not awareness. It was kind of hidden or pushed under the rug . . . But now, I think it is coming to the forefront because there are so many advocators who've decided to advocate for women's rights and bring them to some type of reform issues and acts that will help them as they deal with these very intimate and private and sometimes violent situations.[30]

The focus groups revealed that they experienced passivity, taboo, secrecy, voicelessness, being hidden, and a lack of transparency and accountability. Study participants also believe that church leaders, particularly in the Pentecostal denomination, are not reporting abuse to authorities when it is reported to the church. The topic of mandated reporters also surfaced. The data also revealed barriers to increasing awareness in the church. Such data included the lack of education about IPV and resources, how women are valued, being dependent on the church denomination and reformation, tithes, and offerings, apologetics in the forgiveness offered to the abuser and praying about the abuse, abusers in church leadership, and a viewpoint that the church is not a safe place for victims and survivors of IPV.

Participant 1 stated, "I personally feel like those that are victims don't always find a safe place in the church to be able to share the trauma that they are experiencing." Participant 3 expressed that the church is "afraid of maybe tithes walking out the door because we may come to the realization that some of our biggest benefactors in the church are also abusers."

However, some study participants indicated that the church is a safe place and has ministries that address trauma and IPV:

> We have done a lot of trauma-informed care work, pre-COVID. Our services looked a little different during COVID because a lot of our services are done outside now where we don't have one-on-one in-person counseling anymore, but . . . we had a licensed

---

30. Dr. Susie C. Owens, interviewed by Bridget P. Robinson, Washington, D.C., March 9, 2022.

clinical social worker here, so she would help us be informed, do trauma-informed training with our staff and our volunteers.[31]

Some study participants recommended that church leaders partner with IPV advocates and law enforcement agencies for IPV interventions. A women's ministry leader and survivor of IPV shares:

> I think it's going to take effective partnerships. I think that the church has to expand their partnership base with the law enforcement agencies and allow law enforcement to come into the church, host more awareness, bring the awareness through law enforcement, bring law enforcement in, maybe have panel discussions, not just in domestic violence month, but throughout the year. So, I think the church has to expand its partnership base.[32]

Participants expressed a range of views on involving law enforcement in addressing IPV. Some saw value in increased collaboration, suggesting year-round awareness efforts and community partnerships involving police involvement. Others, however, voiced concern that law enforcement is often ill-equipped to respond effectively in African American communities, where mistrust of police is rooted in historical and ongoing injustices. One Christian worker stated, "Our community, I would say, doesn't, for obvious reason, does not trust law enforcement."[33] The participants shared ideas for how the church and law enforcement can foster trust with victims of IPV by creating safe spaces for community conversations, engaging in IPV outreach awareness activities year-round, developing a community resource guide for victims of IPV, and advocacy training for church leaders and law enforcement officers.

The study participants collectively communicated a need to merge psychological, emotional, and spiritual components of ministry. During an interview, a professional counselor stated, "I think, many times, when individuals become part of a ministry or become part of a church, even accept Christ, they automatically assume all their problems are going to be over."[34]

31. Mallory Zimmerman, interviewed by Bridget P. Robinson, Baltimore, MD, February 18, 2022.

32. Study Participant 2, observed by Bridget P. Robinson. Focus Group 2, Washington, D.C., February 22, 2022.

33. Mallory Zimmerman, interviewed by Bridget P. Robinson, Baltimore, MD, February 18, 2022.

34. Dawn C. Crump, M.Ed., LPC, interviewed by Bridget P. Robinson, Rockhill, SC, March 5, 2022.

When that expectation isn't met, they may struggle in silence or feel spiritually inadequate, highlighting the need for churches to provide more specific emotional and psychological support alongside spiritual care. All participants recommended trauma-informed care training for church leaders. Several participants referenced misinterpreting the Scriptures, such as Eph 5:22–24, "wives submit," indicating a need for correct hermeneutics and exegesis. During a focus group, a survivor shared, "I actually had a pastor, the pastor, the church I was at, even though I was coming in with a black eye, [say], 'submit unto to your husband,' [like] I was not in submission to my husband as being the head of my household."

These focus groups and interviews substantiate that the clergy may not understand the impact of IPV on their parishioners and the community they serve. They provide a scaffolding for developing an IPV intervention curriculum for the clergy as well future studies in trauma-informed theology.

Adverse Childhood Experience Questionnaire Analysis

The Adverse Childhood Experience (ACE) self-report ten-question measuring tool identifies early abuse and neglect that correlate early trauma with impairments in social, emotional, and cognitive development. This research set a goal of one hundred ACE questionnaires to be completed by African American women over the age of eighteen. Prior to the commencement of the survey, the volunteer study participants were presented with the following message: "These questions may cause distress. Some questions ask directly about experiences of child abuse. Check that you have a support person or helpline number available before beginning. You can also call Trauma Resource Center 1-800-662-4357." The ACE questionnaire was self-administered online to fifty-eight African American women volunteers who clicked on the Google link provided to them. The volunteers were asked if they were exposed to the following eight ACE items: physical, emotional, or sexual abuse, household mental illness, incarceration, substance use, domestic violence, parental separation, or divorce. The study participants originated from several states in metropolitan areas within California, Delaware, the District of Columbia, Florida, Maryland, Missouri, New York, North Carolina, South Carolina, and Tennessee. The final analysis of the responses is shown below.

- Twenty-three study participants had an ACE score of four or more,

- Eight study participants had an ACE score of three,
- Four study participants had an ACE score of two,
- Twelve study participants had an ACE score of one,
- Eleven study participants had an ACE score of zero.

It is important to note that having an ACE score of four or higher leads to a 4.6-fold rise in depression.[35] There is a doubling of high perceived stress, a quadrupling of trouble managing anger, a 5.5-fold increase in perpetrating IPV, and a 12.1-fold increase in suicide attempts.[36] ACEs have also been linked to a markedly higher risk of experiencing IPV, both as a perpetrator and a victim.[37] Additionally, individuals with a score of four or more ACEs have a 90 percent higher likelihood of developing cancer, a 60 percent increased likelihood of developing diabetes, a 2.2-fold higher risk of ischemic heart disease, a 2.4-fold higher risk of stroke, and a 3.9-fold higher risk of chronic obstructive pulmonary disease.[38]

The ACE survey serves as an excellent intervention tool for the church to gain a comprehensive understanding of the demographic characteristics of its parishioners, with a specific focus on women. Women have a significantly greater probability than men to disclose a range of ACEs, as well as encounter mental health, social, and emotional difficulties in adulthood.[39] In the United States, 21 percent of men and 39 percent of women have encountered several ACEs before reaching the age of 18.[40] This study offers clergy a practical framework for trauma-informed theology for recognizing and responding to IPV within congregations. By embracing these principles, churches can begin building ministries that are safer, more compassionate, and better equipped to support healing in the African American community.

---

35. Felitti et al., "Relationship of Childhood Abuse and Household Dysfunction," 245–58.

36. Anda et al., "The Enduring Effects of Abuse and Related Adverse Experiences in Childhood," 174–86.

37. Whitfield et al., "Violent Childhood Experiences and the Risk of Intimate Partner Violence," 166–85.

38. Felitti et al., "Relationship of Childhood Abuse and Household Dysfunction," 245–58.

39. Haahr-Pedersen, et al., "Females Have More Complex Patterns of Childhood Adversity."

40. Haahr-Pedersenet et al., "Females Have More Complex Patterns of Childhood Adversity."

Trauma-Informed Theology Theologians Interview Analysis

Preachers need proper training in hermeneutics, homiletics, apologetics in prayer, and forgiveness to mitigate retraumatizing individuals who have experienced trauma. Interviewees gave credence to the need for trauma-informed theology:

> It is about being really careful with language and prayers. Just trying to choose words that are sensitive and respectful of those who have experienced trauma and to avoid retraumatizing with violent imagery or hierarchical language.[41]

> I think that sin is often truncated [in] very kind of black-and-white ways, and there's such a focus on the perpetrator being forgiven and getting a second chance that there isn't an understanding of the one who has been sinned against.[42]

Travis proposes the utilization of Bibliodrama as a potential technique. She references *Scripture Windows* (1997), the literary work of Peter A. Pitzele, to define Bibliodrama. "Bibliodrama is a form of role-playing or improvisation, that invites people to interact with the Bible stories for the purposes of education, community building, and therapy."[43] Additionally, she explores the concept of lamentation as a hermeneutical framework that facilitates a trauma-informed theological perspective in preaching.[44]

Practical Application of Trauma-Informed Theology

Bishop Thomas Dexter Jakes, a renowned pastor, preacher, and cultural voice, is widely recognized for his ability to merge theological depth with emotional and spiritual sensitivity from the pulpit. Frank Thomas argues that people come to church "to receive from the personification of an aspect of the character of God [the preacher] teaching from God's word to steer the hearer in the way of wisdom."[45] Jakes's formula as outlined below achieves personification through the integration of intellectualism and spirituality, which strengthens the position for trauma-informed theology as a praxis to be included in preaching demonstrations of the practical application:

41. Travis, November 10, 2022.
42. Sancken, November 21, 2022.
43. Travis, *Unspeakable*, Chapter 5, Location 2762. Kindle.
44. Travis, *Unspeakable*, Introduction, Location 311. Kindle.
45. Jakes, *Don't Drop the Mic*, 405.

- Develop the abstract principle from the biblical text and life experience into what might be called a contemporary proverb;
- Move to ensure the beauty of proverb for the hearer (adornment);
- Illustrate said proverb in the life of the hearer and their relationship (drama);
- Direct, prompt, and request call and the response of the audience;
- Receive the "movement of presence" from God; and
- The Holy Spirit leads the people to connect with God and live out the biblically contextualized proverb.[46]

In this framework, transformation runs deep. It's not just about being moved emotionally; it's about a renewal of both heart and mind. Bishop T.D. Jakes preaches with a power that does more than motivate. It wakes something up inside. His message, anchored in the gospel of Jesus Christ, speaks directly to those who are hurting, offering real hope, healing, and the strength to rise again. When he preaches, you feel invited to see yourself differently, to reclaim your God-given dignity, and to walk in the kind of freedom that leads to healing not just for the individual, but for the whole community.

Two sermons by Bishop Jakes profoundly speak to the four Rs of trauma-informed theology: *"Surviving the Trauma of Rejection and Abandonment"* and *"Trauma, Triggers, and Triumph,"* both preached at The Potter's House in Dallas. In these sermons, Bishop Jakes names the presence of trauma, affirms the pain of those who have suffered, responds with empathy and truth, and uses language that honors rather than harms. The sermons spoke to the impacts of trauma, such as rejection, abandonment, sexual abuse, sudden death, and violence, in his ministry context and culture. Jakes says:

> The reason why the room is quiet is because almost every person in here has some sort of story that I just triggered, and you have the trauma and the rejection and the abandonment, but you ain't [sic] got no plan. So, you buried what you couldn't get rid of, hoping it would go away. This is the problem with the contemporary church because all we want you to do is praise. In the old church, we used to wail. Even in the Baptist church, we had a mourner's bench.[47]

---

46. Jakes, *Don't Drop the Mic*, 403–4.
47. Jakes, "Surviving the Trauma of Rejection and Abandonment Plan."

Jakes' sermons recognize the signs and symptoms of trauma and mental health challenges. His sermons encourage the listener to acknowledge their trauma, rejection, and abandonment issues and to open their mouth to get their story of trauma out for the healing to begin. The sermons also used traumatic Bible stories such as Tamar being raped by her brother Amnon (2 Sam 13:4–22) and the rejection and persecution of Jesus Christ. Jakes says:

> Open your mouth; do not sit there with your mouth glued together and let your soul explode in unexpressed agony. God wants to ventilate the trauma that has attacked your soul. [. . .] We have been silent too long. It's okay not to be okay.[48]

> There is something about wailing before God that is more therapeutic than therapy. It is a mechanism down in your soul that releases living water so that the stench of what you've been through cannot stagnate inside of you. Open your mouth and shout to God.[49]

After careful analysis of the sermons by Jakes, the 4Rs (realization, recognizing, responding, and resisting retraumatization) of the trauma-informed care framework were evident.

1. Realize—The sermons realize the impact of trauma in their ministry context and culture, such as rejection, abandonment, sexual abuse, sudden death, and violence.

2. Recognize—The sermons recognize signs and symptoms of trauma and mental health challenges.

3. Respond—The sermons encourage the listener to acknowledge their trauma, rejection, and abandonment issues and to open their mouth to get their story of trauma out for the healing to begin.

4. Resisting Retraumatization—Both sermons suggest that the listeners plan to survive trauma, have a healthy theology of God, recommend therapy, and find a safe and healthy church that talks about trauma. The personification of Jakes's preaching, which includes both intellectualism and spirituality, may act as a protective barrier for survivors of trauma who receive his message, shielding them from further pain.

---

48. Jakes, "Trauma, Triggers, and Triumph."
49. Jakes, "Surviving the Trauma of Rejection and Abandonment Plan."

These sermons showed me it's possible to hold space for healing in the pulpit and model what it means to minister with care, wisdom, and accountability. These sermons serve as models for preachers to consider their congregations' social and cultural contexts when crafting sermons that incorporate trauma-informed theology.

Trauma-Informed Theology: Theoretical Framework for IPV Curriculum

> "The Spirit of the Lord is upon me, because he hath anointed me to preach the gospel to the poor; he hath sent me to heal the brokenhearted, to preach deliverance to the captives . . . to set at liberty them that are bruised." —Luke 4:18 (KJV)

This sacred calling laid out in Luke 4:18 is the heartbeat of trauma-informed ministry. As Baldwin insightfully observes, "we as a society are living more in our threat responses,"[50] triggering fear, increasing violence, and deepening the impact of social and cultural trauma. "Trauma seeps into the very groundwater of our cultural awareness."[51]

This reality underscores the pressing need for a theological framework that equips us to respond with spiritual depth and cultural awareness. For clergy serving in African American Pentecostal contexts, this approach is not just helpful; it is a vital and immediate necessity.

In response, a culturally competent curriculum has been developed grounded in trauma-informed theology and attuned to the lived experiences of African American women facing IPV. It offers practical tools and Holy Spirit-inspired strategies for pastoral care, instructional planning, training, and ongoing ministry development. By drawing on adult learning theories and best practices in cultural competency, the curriculum provides a comprehensive framework for equipping leaders to recognize risk factors, resist retraumatization, and respond with clarity and compassion.

What follows is not just a training tool; it's a ministry resource, a blueprint for transformational care, and a call to teach, preach, heal, and set free. It's an opportunity to make a profound difference in the lives of those we serve.

---

50. Baldwin, "Trauma-Sensitive Theology."
51. Baldwin, "Trauma-Sensitive Theology."

4

Resist Retraumatization

Shepherding Through Education: A Theological Framework for Trauma-Informed Curriculum Implementation

THE SPIRIT OF THE Lord is calling us to act. Guided by Luke 4:18, this curriculum equips Pentecostal clergy to respond faithfully and effectively to IPV within African American communities. I built this curriculum on a trauma-informed theological foundation intentionally shaped by the lived realities of African American women, pastoral experience, and insights from leading trauma-informed theologians. It actively confronts the silence and stigma surrounding IPV by integrating biblical truth, cultural competency, and Spirit-empowered care. This is not just a resource. It's a call to shepherd with wisdom and courage. Let us answer this call and make a difference in our communities.

Learning Objectives and Expected Outcomes

By the end of this intensive training curriculum, you will achieve the following objectives:

1. Enhance your understanding of the distinct risk factors associated with IPV within the African American community, particularly among African American women.
2. Help clergy members understand and apply effective intervention strategies to address IPV in their roles as leaders and within their congregations.

3. Offer comprehensive resources and information about IPV.
4. Foster an understanding of trauma-informed theology.

These goals will be accomplished by implementing the principles of "trauma-informed theology" through the four Rs of trauma-informed care:

- Realize the widespread impact of trauma.
- Recognize the signs and symptoms of trauma.
- Respond by fully integrating knowledge about trauma into policies, procedures, and practices.
- Resist retraumatization.

These principles serve as the framework for the curriculum.

Facilitating the Curriculum

This curriculum is designed to be completed over four to five days, and I strongly recommend that a skilled facilitator guide the sessions to help set the tone and pace in ways that address ministry or organization unique needs and goals. While it's ideal to hold these sessions in person, allowing participants to have more connectivity with the content and one another, they can also be delivered virtually using platforms like Zoom, if needed. That said, the material is flexible enough for individuals to engage independently when a facilitator is unavailable.

For group facilitation, I suggest having the following supplies on hand to support participation and creativity throughout the training:

- Name tags
- Bibles
- Flip chart paper
- Easel
- Markers
- Projector and screen
- Laptop computers (for both facilitator and participants)
- PowerPoint slide deck (optional, can be created by the facilitator)
- Pens and pencils

- VGA or HDMI cable (if needed)
- Glue sticks
- Magazines (for visual exercises)
- Poster paper

These basic tools will help create a dynamic, engaging environment for participants to reflect, share, and begin shaping trauma-informed theology practices that can transform ministry from the inside out.

Recommended Daily Schedule for Training (8:00 a.m. to 4 p.m.):

Arrive—8:00 a.m.

Instructional Time—8:30 a.m. to 10 a.m.

Break—10 a.m. to 10:15 a.m.

Instructional Time—10:15 a.m. to 12 p.m.

Lunch – 12 p.m. to 1:00 p.m.

Instructional Time—1:00 p.m. to 2:30 p.m.

Break – 2:30 p.m. to 2:45 p.m.

Instructional Time—2:45 p.m. to 3:45 p.m.

Exit Ticket (Formative Assessment Tool)—3:45 p.m. to 4:00 p.m.

Curriculum Theoretical Framework

I think it is important for you, as leaders of the church, to know the theoretical framework for the development and design of the African American IPV curriculum because it may be the first of its kind specifically for the Pentecostal clergy. Only a few studies focus on the problem of IPV among African American women in Pentecostal ministry in the US, compared to more studies evaluating IPV in African Pentecostalism in Africa. Further research and comparison studies are needed in the US to include the African diaspora for culturally specific IPV intervention tools for the clergy. While this curriculum is rooted explicitly in the experiences of African American Pentecostal communities, its trauma-informed approach offers a model that can be adapted and applied in other cultural and ministry contexts to raise awareness of IPV globally.

The curriculum is built around four key modules—Realization, Recognition, Response, and Resist Retraumatization, the 4Rs of trauma-informed care. These form the foundation of trauma-informed theology and guide the curriculum flow thoughtfully and step-by-step. Each module includes clear goals, practical application, and actionable steps. Using Bloom's Taxonomy, a framework that categorizes levels of cognitive learning from basic knowledge to higher-order thinking, lessons are shaped to ensure that learning objectives, outcomes, and assessments are meaningfully aligned and easy to follow.[1]

Understanding adult learning principles is paramount to instructional design. Malcolm Knowles proposed an Andragogy Theory of Learning for adult learners. The andragogy theory suggests that adults are mostly independent learners, self-directed and self-motivated, seek immediate benefit in real-life situations, and use their own life experiences to learn.[2] Adults acquire knowledge and skills through the utilization of three main learning methods: visual media, such as photographs, movies; text and auditory, such as lectures and podcasts; and kinesthetic, which involves using activities, role play, and group tasks to facilitate the learning process. This curriculum integrates the five pillars and four adult learning principles outlined by Malcolm Knowles.[3,4,5]

---

1. Bloom, ed., *Taxonomy of Educational Objectives*.
2. Kumar, "Adult Learning and Instructional Design Model for Trainers."
3. Blevins, "Learning Styles: The Impact on Education," 285–86.
4. Knowles, *Andragogy in Action*.
5. Valamis, "Learning Theories, Adult Learning Principles."

Trauma-Informed Theology

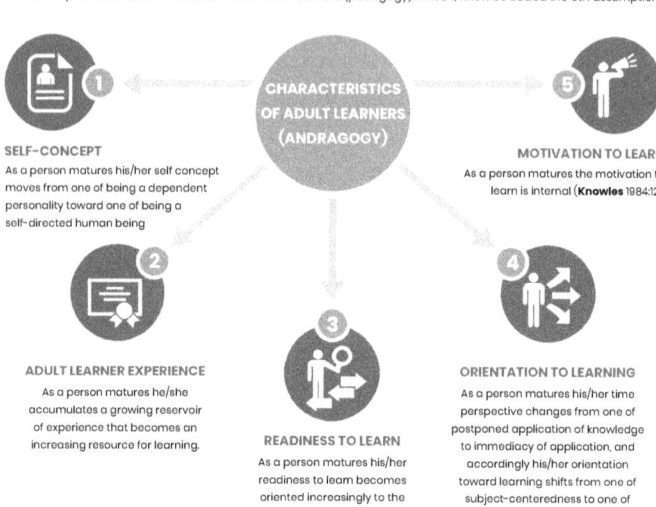

Figure 15. Knowles's 5 Assumptions of Adult Learners[6]

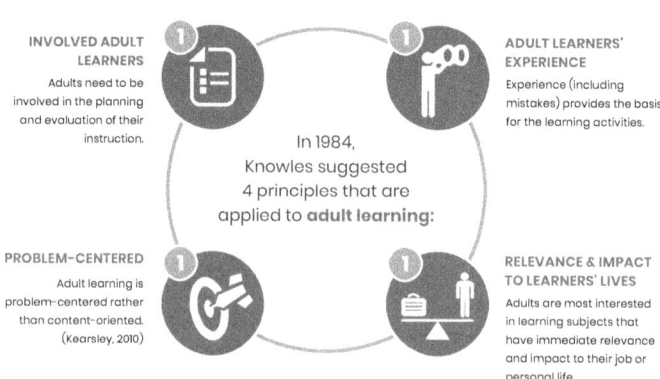

Figure 16. Knowles's 4 Principles of Andragogy[7]

6. Elearning Infographics, "Knowles' 5 Assumptions of Adult Learners," accessed October 28, 2023, https://elearninginfographics.com/adult-learning-theory-andragogy-infographic/.

7. Elearning Infographics, "The Adult Learning Theory—Andragogy—Infographic,"

African American Cultural Competency

Washington says, "Cultural competency is not something you can tell someone you have; it is something that is experience."[8]

Cultural competency refers to the understanding and recognition of one's perspective on the world and the ability to value and comprehend the experiences of people affected by trauma. Developing cultural competency is essential for establishing an atmosphere that promotes effective learning, understanding, and communication with individuals from diverse cultural backgrounds.

Cross's Six Stages of Cultural Competency provides an outline of the matriculation of one moving along a continuum to becoming culturally competent and continual growth:

1. *Cultural Destructiveness* refers to the detrimental impact on a cultural group resulting from the dominant group's attitudes, policies, institutions, and practices that are deeply ingrained inside a system or organization.
2. *Cultural Incapacity* refers to the inherent inability of institutions and organizations to effectively address the unique demands and requirements of culturally and linguistically diverse people.
3. *Cultural Blindness* refers to treating all individuals similarly, disregarding their cultural backgrounds and unique identities.
4. *Cultural Pre-Competence* is essential for individuals to acquire in order to adequately address the needs of culturally and linguistically diverse populations, institutions, and organizations. This involves awareness of one's strengths and areas that require additional growth.
5. *Cultural Competency* refers to the recognition and appreciation of cultural variety within systems and organizations and the demonstration of competence in incorporating cultural sensitivity into their practices.
6. *Cultural Proficiency* is a concept that recognizes culture as the central element in the pursuits of all systems and organizations. The

---

accessed October 28, 2023, https://elearninginfographics.com/adult-learning-theory-andragogy-infographic/.

8. Washington, "African American Cultural Competency Training Program."

organization's projects, policies, and governance are all guided by this principle. [9]

I had the privilege to interview Tselane Gardner, an expert in cultural competency and African American mental health. Gardner references the *Seven Psychological Strengths of African Americans* by Dr. Joseph L. White as a framework for designing and developing a culturally competent African American IPV curriculum:

1. *Improvisation* refers to the ability to exhibit innovative thinking and effectively utilize available resources when confronted with problems;

2. *Resilience* refers to the psychological and emotional fortitude that enables individuals to recover and rebound from various forms of adversity, encompassing both physical and mental challenges, as well as spiritual distress;

3. *Connectedness to Others* refers to the process of building interpersonal bonds, which is enhanced by being in the presence of other individuals;

4. *Spirituality* is aligned with the Black experience, promoting resilience and fostering hope;

5. *Emotional Vitality* refers to the presence of heightened energy levels within the domains of music, church, and community;

6. *Gallows Humor* refers to the ability to find humor in challenging or distressing circumstances;

7. *Healthy Suspicion of You Know Who* refers to a healthy suspicion of people with a history of broken promises and mistreatment since 1619.[10]

It is important to acknowledge that the curriculum incorporates a combination of African Adinkra symbols. The term "Adinkra" refers to a linguistic expression employed by the Asante community in the Twi language, denoting a message conveyed to another individual upon departure, akin to the English term "farewell" or "goodbye."[11] The origin of the Adinkra symbols can be traced to West Africa, and they are intertwined with the African diaspora. Approximately 50 percent of the enslaved Africans

---

9. Cross et al., "A Monograph on Effective Services for Minority Children," 1–90.
10. Metta Healing Oasis, "The Seven Psychological Strengths of African Americans."
11. Kissi, et al, "The Philosophy of Adinkra Symbols," 29–39.

brought to the US were from western Africa.[12] During the height of the Atlantic slave trade, roughly one out of every six West Africans sold into slavery came from this region.[13]

The Adinkra iconography conveys historical and cultural significance through many mediums, such as textiles, pottery, and metalwork. This deliberate selection of symbols aims to help participants engaging with the curriculum to be cognizant of the African origins of the African American community and the culturally diverse heritage of the African diaspora. Furthermore, these symbols serve as a reminder of the need for healing from intergenerational trauma and the various forms of trauma experienced by African American women, particularly in the context of IPV. The African Adinkra symbols' name and meanings follow:

Gye Nyame, meaning "except for God," symbolizes God's omnipotence through the knowledge that people should not fear anything except God.[14]

Figure 17. "Gye Nyame" African Adinkra Symbol

Nsoromma, which translates to "children of the heavens" or "star," serves as a symbol representing the divine guardianship of God and his omnipresent watchfulness over all living entities.[15]

---

12. Pruitt, "What Part of Africa Did Most Enslaved People Come From?"
13. Pruitt, "What Part of Africa Did Most Enslaved People Come From?"
14. National Park Service, "Gye Nyame—Supremacy of God."
15. National Park Service, "Nsoromma—Guardianship."

Figure 18. "Nsoromma," African Adinkra Symbol

Matie Masie means "what I hear, I keep." The emblem of four linked ears reminds individuals to listen and communicate, especially in oral cultures. It represents wisdom and knowledge through good judgment and insight.[16]

Figure 19. "Matie Masie," African Adinkra Symbol

Akoma ntoso means "linked hearts." The emblem shows four hearts intertwined, symbolizing soul immortality and sympathy. Akoma ntoso also unites families and communities.[17]

---

16. National Park Service, "Matie Masie—Wisdom and Prudence."
17. National Park Service, "Akoma Ntoso—Understanding."

Figure 20. "Akoma Ntoso," African Adinkra Symbol

Denkyem means "crocodile." This Adinkra symbol is about adaptability because the crocodile can breathe air even though it lives in swamps and water. During the Transatlantic slave trade, enslaved Africans were taken from their homes in Africa and put in a place they did not know. This symbol is for all the Africans of the diaspora.[18]

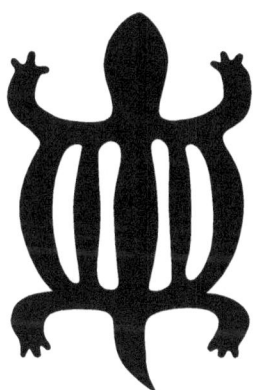

Figure 21. "Denkyem," African Adinkra Symbol

Sankofa is a communication technique and a symbol. The symbol's iconography communicates the phrase "Look to the past to guide the future," which can be interpreted as drawing insights and lessons from historical events and experiences to influence future actions and decisions. Slavery is vital to the African American narrative, and it is imperative for society to flourish.[19]

---

18. National Park Service, "Denkyem—Adaptability."
19. National Park Service, "Sankofa—Learn from the Past."

Figure 22. "Sankofa," African Adinkra Symbol

Using this program will enhance cultural competency, allowing clergy to get a more profound understanding of the risk factors linked to IPV among African American women. Clergy members are expected to develop a heightened understanding of IPV and trauma-informed theology. Engagement with the curriculum may lead to several outcomes, such as the development of self-assurance in utilizing the skills offered to address IPV in the congregation and the ability to advocate for trauma-informed policies and procedures within church organizations. Consequently, this engagement has the potential to foster the creation of secure environments that support survivors and victims of trauma and IPV. The individual can implement trauma-informed theology by employing the 4Rs of trauma-informed care. These newly acquired insights are considered essential components that will be used in their ministry initiatives.

The curriculum considers African Americans' worldview in the context of their culture. It intentionally incorporates African American perspectives to promote cultural awareness and sensitivity, creating an IPV curriculum that honors the lived experiences of African Americans, including their language, symbols, values, spiritual beliefs, and ways of being, within a Pentecostal context.

Standards of Publication

The Dick and Carey and ADDIE Instructional Design Models supported the development of the curriculum. In 1978 Walter Dick, Lou Carey, and James Carey developed the Dick and Carey Model. The Dick and Carey Model has a ten-step systematic approach and is more appropriate in educational settings than corporate. This model helps determine the lesson's scope and sequence and how to teach it. This model focuses more on design than the ADDIE Model.

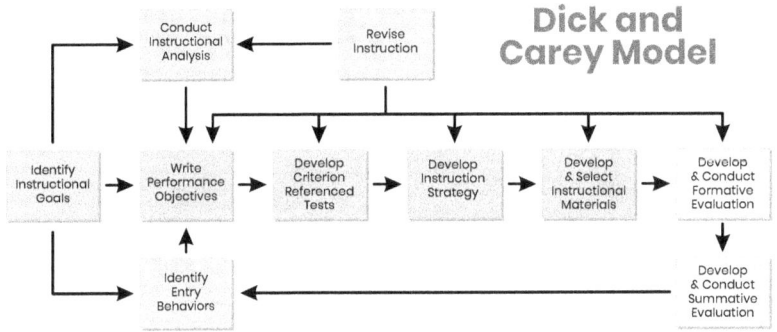

Figure 23. Dick and Carey Model for Instructional Design[20]

ADDIE is an acronym for analysis, design, development, implementation, and evaluation. Curriculum development should align training objectives with the organization's strategic objective, i.e., trauma-informed ministry. The training plan is guided by the ADDIE model, which shapes its development through five key components: Analysis, Design, Development, Implementation, and Evaluation.

- A purpose statement
- An overview of the target audience
- Design assumptions
- Training process
- Evaluation measures

20. Kurt, "Dick and Carey Instructional Model."

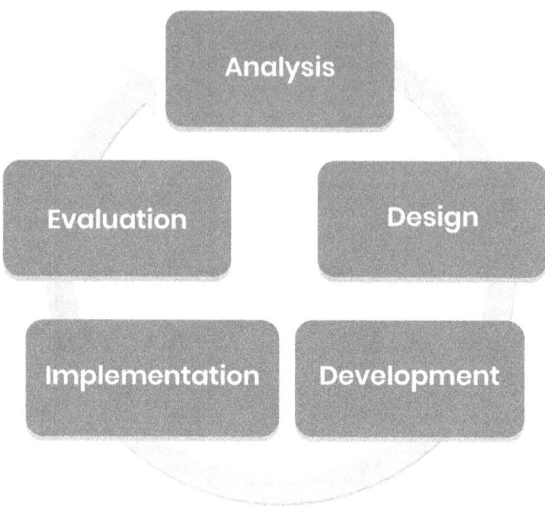

Figure 24. ADDIE Training and Curriculum Development[21]

The models presented a comprehensive framework for developing a curriculum prototype, including instructional planning, training, adult learning theories, curriculum design, production, and evaluations. Furthermore, these models provide recommendations for developing cultural competency and promoting comprehension of trauma-informed theology and IPV. These variables are of utmost importance when devising the framework and advancement of IPV interventions for religious communities.

The scope and sequence are adapted from Thomas H. Groome's Shared Christian Praxis Model[22] into a trauma-informed clergy curriculum.

---

21. Kurt, "Addie Model: Instructional Design."
22. Groome, *Sharing Faith*, 146–48.

Scope and Sequence: Trauma-Informed Theology: An African American Intimate Partner Violence Intervention Tool for the Pentecostal Clergy

Movement	Focus	Instructional Activities	Intended Outcomes
1. Present Action	Naming current realities and ministry responses to IPV	Explore the basics of IPV—what it is, how it manifests, and why trauma-informed pastoral care matters centered on the African American experience of Black women. Includes group discussion and action planning.	Cultivate self-awareness of existing theology and ministry practices in relation to IPV and trauma.
2. Critical Reflection	Reexamining theology and Pentecostal practices through a trauma-informed lens	Engage a case study of an African American IPV survivor to explore Pentecostal risk factors, patriarchy, and intersectionality. Includes guided reflection and an action step.	Deepen theological understanding and begin reframing ministry for healing and justice.
3. Making the Story Our Own	Connecting biblical healing to communal transformation	Examine types of trauma, trauma-informed care, and cultural competency in understanding IPV among African American women. Activities include role-playing, group discussion, theological reflection, an action step.	Integrate trauma-informed theology with Pentecostal identity, recognizing the Holy Spirit's work in restoration.
4. Discernment to Praxis	Creating trauma-informed action and sustaining transformed ministry	Draft trauma-informed policies (e.g., altar calls, testimonies, counseling); develop IPV awareness sermons; practice safe pastoral responses to disclosures; implement teachings in ministry settings. Peer feedback, reflection, and an action step.	Equip clergy to lead with wisdom and conviction, creating healing-centered church communities committed to "do no harm."

With a strong theological foundation and culturally responsive framework now in place, the time has come to move from vision to action. This curriculum was not created to sit on a shelf. It is meant to be lived out in pulpits, classrooms, counseling sessions, and everyday ministry. As clergy, we are called to shepherd God's people with knowledge and compassion, especially in the places where pain has been ignored or misunderstood. Implementing this curriculum is an act of faithful leadership. It is a commitment to see, respond, and cultivate healing communities rooted in the love of Christ. What follows are the steps, strategies, and resources to begin this vital work. Remember, you are not alone in this journey. Support and guidance are always available. Let us walk forward as ministers of the gospel and as agents of transformation.

MODULE ONE

Realize

Module 1: Realize (Day 1)

We begin by **realizing** the widespread impact of trauma, particularly within the African American community. This module not only explores the spiritual, psychological, and social realities of intimate partner violence (IPV) but also emphasizes the need for a better understanding of its roots, such as systemic racism, historical oppression, and patriarchy. You will be invited to see through a new lens: one that truly respects and values lived experience, Scripture, and the healing work of the Holy Spirit, empowering you with a comprehensive understanding of trauma.

By the end of this module, participants will:

- Define and recognize the signs and symptoms of IPV.
- Identify historical and cultural factors contributing to the prevalence of IPV in African American communities.
- Reflect on how their personal and pastoral context may influence their awareness of trauma and IPV.

Focus Activity

Movement 1—Present Action: Naming current realities and ministry responses to IPV

Opening Prayer

Heavenly Father, who has created all things for your glory, we, your children, stand before you. We acknowledge that both men and women are made in your image and likeness, and we thank you for the goodness of your creation. We understand that there is no hierarchy in your perfect creation of humanity. We pray for the wisdom, knowledge, and understanding to realize the impact of trauma and to increase our awareness of intimate partner violence in all communities, especially for African American women. We recognize our role in this, and we will be teachable and let your Holy Spirit lead us in the ways of the Lord that will bring about healing, deliverance, and wholeness in our sanctuary, pews, and communities.

In the name of your son Jesus Christ, we pray.
Amen.

Icebreaker

Participants will state their name and share what the Bible verse and African proverb for Module 1 means to them.

Scripture

> Who is wise? Let them **realize** these things. Who is discerning? Let them understand. The ways of the Lord are right; the righteous walk in them, but the rebellious stumble in them. —Hos 14:19

What does this Bible verse mean to me?

In your role as clergy, how do you discern when a victim of IPV is walking in obedience to God by seeking safety, even when that choice disrupts traditional views on marriage or submission? It is crucial to understand the victim's perspective in these situations.

Hosea's words, that "the rebellious stumble" in the ways of the Lord, serve as a reminder. How might certain theological beliefs or church practices, when left unexamined, contribute to a victim's sense of guilt, shame, or hesitation about leaving an abusive relationship? And more importantly, how can you, as clergy, walk in wisdom and compassion to prevent this kind of harm?

_____

_____

_____

_____

_____

African Proverb

> "No matter how beautiful and well-crafted a coffin might look, it will not make anyone wish for death." —African proverb

What is the meaning of this African proverb?

This proverb reminds us that no one truly desires death, no matter how dignified it may appear. How can we, as spiritual leaders, ensure we are not unintentionally glorifying suffering, such as encouraging victims to stay in harmful relationships for the sake of appearances, doctrine, or community expectations?

In your pastoral care, how do you recognize when a survivor's cry for help is being hidden behind the "well-crafted coffin" of silence, shame, or religious duty? What can you do to affirm their instinct for life, safety, and dignity?

_____
_____
_____
_____
_____
_____

Warm-up Activity: "Glory" A Reflection on Collective and Personal Strength

This warm-up activity is designed to help you connect with the workshop themes and prepare for the reflective activity that follows. As we begin this sacred space of learning, healing, and reflection, we invite you to listen deeply to the song "Glory" by Common and John Legend. If you do not have the song readily available, you can download it from a music app or listen on YouTube.

This anthem was born from struggle and hope—a mirror of the African American journey through injustice, resistance, and the enduring pursuit of freedom. In this shared experience, we are all part of a collective journey of reflection and healing.

Instructions

While listening, we ask you to sit in stillness and let the music speak not just to your ears but to your mind, body, and spirit. As the lyrics unfold, consider:

- What emotions are rising in you?
- What physical sensations or reactions do you notice?
- What thoughts or memories are surfacing personally, communally, spiritually?

Now, take a few moments to write freely. Reflect on:

- How the song makes you feel in your mind, body, and spirit.

- Any symbols, images, or memories that come to mind, whether of struggle, silence, resistance, or rising.

Feel free to express yourself in any way that feels right for you. You may write in sentences, draw a symbol, or list words. This is your space for free expression.

Sharing (Optional)

Afterward, you are invited to share your reflections with the group; however, this is entirely optional. This is a space of non-judgment, collective care, and sacred storytelling. Through your voice, we honor the stories of survival, strength, and spiritual resilience woven into the African American experience, especially those impacted by IPV.

_____
_____
_____
_____
_____
_____

Module 1—Intimate Partner Violence

This section introduces key terms and theoretical frameworks for understanding IPV, particularly as it affects African American women. Students will engage with clear, practical definitions to help them grasp the realities of IPV within a ministry context.

What Is IPV?

Throughout this training, it is essential to have a comprehensive and gender-specific definition of IPV. IPV, for this context, is any form of intentional abuse or intimidation as an attempt to maintain power and control and oppressive systems against another by willfully engaging in acts of violence, coercion, and restricting the freedom of another, including physical, sexual, psychological, economic, spiritual, and digital. This definition integrates the terms domestic violence and gender-based violence.

Defining the Problem of IPV

One in four women experience IPV, a staggering statistic that underscores the urgent need for understanding and addressing this issue among ministry leaders.[23] It is imperative to note the higher rate of IPV in the African American community in the United States.

- 45.1 percent of Black women
- 37.3 percent of White women
- 34.4 percent of Hispanic women
- and 18.3 percent of Asian women will experience IPV.[24]

These IPV rates underscore the urgent need for education and awareness. Clergy leaders may not be fully aware of the profound impact on women, especially on African American women. Increasing your understanding of IPV is not just knowledge; it is a life-saving tool. It opens the door to healing, deliverance, and prevention, breaking generational abuse and oppressive systems.

What are the local (county) statistics for IPV in your state? You can research this information online.

_____

_____

Patriarchal Structures Are Rooted in Power and Control

Patriarchal systems create a culture of male dominance over women and children and the marginalized in society. This system, and how men gain and maintain power and control of women, is best illustrated in Duluth's Models of Power and Control, a comprehensive framework that highlights each spoke of the wheel and how this is accomplished.

---

23. Centers for Disease Control and Prevention. "Fast Facts."

24. Smith, et al. "The National Intimate Partner and Sexual Violence Survey," 117–118.

Figure 25. Power and Control Wheel[25]

Patriarchal systems are not only prevalent in our society, but this hierarchical structure is also evident in the church.

25. https://www.theduluthmodel.org/wp-content/uploads/2017/03/PowerandControl.pdf

Resist Retraumatization

Figure 26. Christian Power and Control Wheel[26]

Kaleidoscope of Abuse—What Are the Symptoms of IPV?

Think of how a kaleidoscope can change its imaging and texture. IPV, too, includes various forms: physical, sexual, psychological, economic, spiritual, and digital. When looking through the kaleidoscope, what do these multiple forms of IPV look like to you?

---

26. https://www.theduluthmodel.org/wp-content/uploads/2023/01/CMCL-PC.pdf

Physical

What does physical abuse look like to you?

Sexual

What does sexual abuse look like to you?

Psychological

What does psychological abuse look like to you?

Verbal

Mental

Emotional

Isolation

Economic

What does economic abuse look like to you?
_____
_____
_____

Spiritual

What does spiritual abuse look like to you?
_____
_____
_____

Digital

What does digital abuse look like to you?
_____
_____
_____

The Cycle of Abuse

The cycle of abuse is a social construct developed by Lenore E. Walker in 1979. IPV escalation can occur over a short or long period, transitioning from psychological and physical to sexual. The recurring cyclical pattern of IPV includes the Tension-Building Phase, Violence Climax Phase, and Moment of Bliss Phase. It's crucial to note that the cycle's pattern is unique to each victim. Still, it does follow a recognizable pattern, which is vital to understanding the predictability of IPV and its potential for escalation. Recognizing and responding to IPV is not only necessary but also essential for the safety and well-being of the victim, underscoring the importance of your role in addressing this issue. The cycle of abuse diagram below is adapted from Walker, 1979.

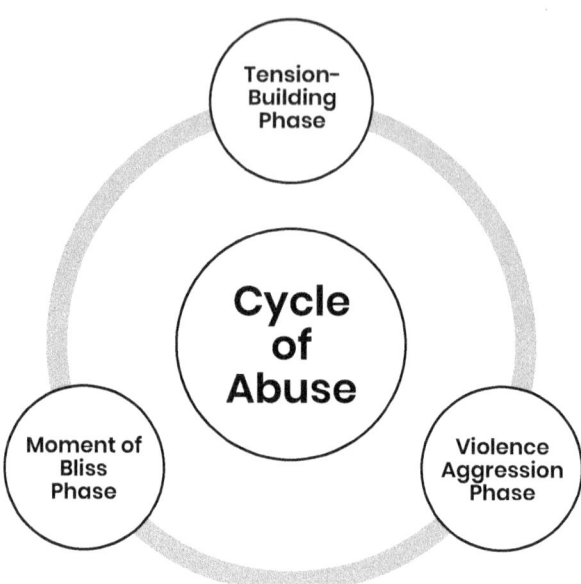

Figure 27. Cycle of Abuse

Tension-Building Phase: The victim often feels as if they are walking on eggshells, as violence can erupt suddenly and unpredictably. The abuser may engage in a range of intimidating behaviors, including criticism, yelling, threats, and humiliation, creating an environment of fear and anxiety for the victim. This unpredictability underscores the urgency of the situation, making it crucial to understand and address it.

Violence Aggression Phase: It is at this point where the abuser executes explosive violence toward the victim to maintain power and control. The abuser abuses the victim physically, emotionally, and/or sexually.

Moment of Bliss Phase: It is the phase after the attack of violence on the victim by the abuser where they show remorse for their behavior by crying, buying gifts, promising to change, asking for forgiveness, or acting as if nothing happened. This phase is designed to confuse the victim and maintain the abuser's control, highlighting the manipulative tactics used. It is important to be aware of these tactics to avoid falling into the abuser's trap. There is a period of calm; the duration of the perceived de-escalation is unpredictable.

The cycle of abuse, therefore, repeats itself constantly with the purpose of the abuser maintaining power and control over the victim and children. The abuser's actions are not random, but rather a calculated strategy to maintain dominance and control.

Discussion Questions

Given the prevalence of abuse in many Pentecostal communities, we must engage in a thoughtful dialogue on this issue.

1. How can Pentecostal theology, which emphasizes deliverance, transformation, and spiritual renewal, be used to support, rather than silence, survivors who are trapped in the cycle of abuse? For instance, can the concept of deliverance be applied to help survivors break free from their abuser's control? Can the emphasis on transformation be used to encourage abusers to change their behavior? Can the focus on spiritual renewal provide a path to healing for survivors?

2. In what ways might traditional teachings on submission, headship, or marital endurance be misinterpreted or misapplied, unintentionally enabling the cycle of abuse within Pentecostal households?

3. How can Pentecostal clergy recognize the emotional, psychological, and spiritual signs of the cycle of abuse even when no physical violence is present and intervene in a way that honors both pastoral care and prophetic justice?

Why Do African American Communities Have Higher Rates of IPV?

The high rates of IPV within the African American community are deeply rooted in the dual legacies of patriarchy and systemic racism. These interlocking systems shape not only personal relationships but also broader institutional responses to violence and trauma. Research shows that 45.1 percent of Black women and 40.1 percent of Black men have experienced IPV, including physical violence, sexual assault, and stalking. Beyond the initial violence, 31 percent of Black women and 16.8 percent of Black men face lasting consequences such as injury, post-traumatic stress, employment disruption, and the need for housing and legal support. These outcomes are not merely individual; they reflect a structural failure to protect Black survivors.[27,28,29]

---

27. Smith et al., "The National Intimate Partner and Sexual Violence Survey," 117–18.

28. Capaldi et al., "A Systematic Review of Risk Factors for Intimate Partner Violence," 231–80.

29. Breiding et al., "Intimate Partner Violence in the United States—2010."

Structural racism significantly influences the socio-economic realities of Black communities, creating conditions that elevate IPV risk. As Blessett and Littleton explain, institutional racism in segregated Black neighborhoods limits access to upward mobility, quality healthcare, stable housing, and education, which are core protective factors against IPV.[30] When systems are not built for equitable access, they indirectly nurture environments where IPV can thrive. Capaldi et al. identify these contextual disadvantages, along with adverse childhood experiences and poverty, as significant risk factors for IPV.[31]

Thus, addressing IPV in Black communities must involve more than individual interventions. It requires systemic change. Compounding the issue is the mistrust between African Americans and law enforcement, a relationship marred by criminalization and disbelief. Jacobs highlights that Black women in particular face "invisible" violence when they turn to the state for protection, only to be arrested or dismissed.[32] The legal system often fails to recognize their trauma, reinforcing a cycle of silence and danger. Black IPV survivors, therefore, encounter unique safety barriers; many are reluctant to report abuse out of fear that the police will not help or, worse, will cause further harm. These social systems of oppression and racial and gendered injustice of IPV must be addressed through culturally competent, trauma-informed policy and practice.

Transformative Conversations

1. How do institutional racism, systemic racism, and patriarchy show up in the stories of IPV survivors within your faith community, particularly in terms of their access to safety, justice, and support?

_____

_____

_____

---

30. Blessett and Littleton, "Examining the Impact of Institutional Racism."

31. Capaldi et al., "A Systematic Review of Risk Factors for Intimate Partner Violence," 231–80.

32. Jacobs, *The Violent State: Black Women's Invisible Struggle Against Police Violence* .

2. In what ways might our religious teachings or practices unintentionally reinforce silence, shame, or disbelief toward Black IPV survivors, especially when they seek help outside traditional institutions like the church or police?

_____
_____
_____

3. Knowing the distrust many Black survivors feel toward law enforcement and the legal system, how can faith leaders become more trusted and trauma-informed advocates who walk alongside survivors on their healing journey?

_____
_____
_____

Exit Ticket

What are three insights or truths that deeply resonated with you today?

_____
_____
_____

What are two ways today's session challenged or expanded your thinking personally, spiritually, or pastorally?

_____
_____
_____

What is one area or question you feel called to explore further as a leader, caregiver, or advocate?

_____
_____
_____

Action Step: From Awareness to Advocacy

As a next step in living out what you've learned, each participant is encouraged to take meaningful action within their sphere of influence. Your actions have the power to make a significant impact on our community. You are invited to:

- Partner with a local domestic/intimate partner violence (IPV/DV) advocacy organization. Your role is crucial in this fight. Whether you volunteer your time, offer support services, or bridge the gap between the faith community and survivor-centered resources, your contribution matters.

- Host an IPV Awareness Event at your church or in your community within the next six months. This could take the form of a prayer vigil, panel discussion, resource fair, healing service, or any other initiative that fosters safety, education, and spiritual support for survivors.

This action step is not simply an assignment; it is a call to embody justice, compassion, and faith in action. Together, as a united front, we can help dismantle silence and build safer, more responsive communities of care.

Personal Journal of Reflection and Prayer

This journal space is an invitation to pause, reflect, and connect with yourself, with God, and with the truths that have emerged during this training. As you write, allow your thoughts, emotions, and prayers to flow freely. There is no right or wrong way to reflect; this is your sacred space for honest dialogue with your soul and your Creator.

You may consider journaling about the following:

- What stirred your spirit during today's session?
- How is God speaking to you about your role in healing and advocacy?
- What past experiences of harm, silence, hope, or strength are surfacing?
- What prayers do you need to pray for yourself, for survivors, or your community?

Take this time to be gentle with yourself. Let your pen become a voice of release, discovery, and prayerful commitment. Remember, healing is a journey, and reflection is a decisive step forward.

MODULE TWO

Recognize

Module 2: Recognize (Day 2)

As shepherds, we must **recognize** the risk factors that prevent clergy from realizing, identifying, and responding to IPV and potentially retraumatizing women victim-survivors of IPV. This module provides practical guidance on recognizing risk factors for IPV within our faith communities, where patriarchal norms and misapplied theology result in hidden silence and shame. By learning to recognize these risk factors in our ministry context, clergy can transition from unawareness to Spirit-led attentiveness, seeing what others overlook and offering hope where despair has prevailed.

By the end of this module, you will:

- Acquire the skills to recognize risk factors in a Pentecostal ministry context. This knowledge will empower you to prevent clergy from overlooking IPV, instead identifying and responding to it, thereby avoiding potential retraumatization of victim-survivors of IPV.
- Be able to analyze patriarchal social contextualization in our culture that enables IPV and your beliefs on male and female gender-role power and control in society.
- Engage in critical reflection on your social reasoning. This process will help you realize, recognize, respond, and resist retraumatizing victim-survivors of IPV in a ministry context.

Focus Activity

Movement 2—Critical Reflection: Reexamining theology and Pentecostal practices through a trauma-informed lens

Opening Prayer

>Abba Father, who is in heaven,

We desire to pattern ourselves after You and bear good fruit, fruit that brings healing, protection, justice, and peace. Today, we come not as ministers but as Your sons and daughters, recognizing that our fruit doesn't always align with Yours. At times, we've prioritized church doctrine, systems, and traditions over the hurting people in our pews. Open our eyes, Lord.

Many women, children, and families in our congregations are suffering, and we confess we haven't always seen them. We may have misunderstood

Your Word, especially around gender roles, headship, and submission. We ask for Your grace and seek divine insight to help us better understand how these beliefs may contribute to harm. The urgency of this issue demands our immediate attention and action.

The Holy Spirit empowers us to recognize the reasoning and blind spots that keep us from truly seeing, responding to, and supporting survivors of intimate partner violence. Help us realize how our words, actions, or silence may retraumatize those who are already wounded. Search our hearts and give us the courage to change.

We want our churches to be safe places, sanctuaries of compassion and refuge. Anoint us afresh to pastor well, not just in the pulpit but in every moment where someone needs protection, dignity, and care. Guide us to create safe spaces for survivors to share their stories, provide resources for them to seek help, and advocate for policies that protect them.

Thank You, Father, for Your transformative power. We trust You to lead us forward, knowing that with Your guidance, we can bring about positive change in our congregations.

Amen.

Icebreaker

Participants share what the Bible verse and African Proverb for Module 2 means to them.

Scripture

> Each tree is **recognized** by its fruit. People do not pick figs from thornbushes or grapes from briars. —Luke 6:44

What does this Bible verse mean to me?

As we hold this Scripture in our hearts, consider the ways Jesus invites us to examine the *fruit*—the visible outcomes—of what we believe, preach, and practice. Suppose our theology is bearing fruit that silences survivors, excuses abuse, or upholds harmful power dynamics. In that case, we must ask: is that the fruit of the Spirit or the fruit of tradition and distortion?

1. When you read, "Each tree is recognized by its fruit," what comes to mind in the context of your ministry?

2. How might the "fruit" of your church's teachings on gender roles (headship, submission, authority) affect those experiencing IPV?

3. Have there been times when theology in your context produced "fruit" that protected image or institution over people's safety and healing? What did that fruit look like?

4. What kind of fruit do you believe the Holy Spirit is calling you to bear in your ministry when it comes to protecting and advocating for victims of IPV?

5. What might need to be pruned or re-rooted in your teaching or leadership to make room for better fruit?

_____
_____
_____
_____
_____
_____
_____
_____
_____
_____
_____

African Proverb

> "There are many colorful flowers on the path of life, but the prettiest have the sharpest thorns." —African proverb

What is the meaning of this African proverb?

This proverb reminds us that not everything that looks good is good. Some things that appear beautiful, such as specific teachings, traditions, or roles within the church, may carry hidden harm.

As pastors and leaders, we know how easy it can be to hold tightly to what looks godly on the surface. But the truth is, some of the things we've embraced, or even taught, about gender roles, marriage, headship, and submission have caused real pain, especially for women, children, and families living with intimate partner violence.

Sometimes, the "sharp thorns" are in the way we spiritualize suffering, telling women to "stay and pray" or prioritizing the image of the church over the safety of the people within it. Sometimes, we don't even realize we're doing it.

This moment is an invitation to pause, reflect, and be honest with God and with ourselves.

1. What does this proverb say to you as a spiritual leader when you think about IPV and the church?
2. Have you ever encountered a teaching or tradition that seemed right but ultimately caused harm to someone?
3. Are there "pretty flowers" in our theology or culture, messages that sound holy but are keeping people silent or stuck?
4. How might we, as clergy, unintentionally carry thorns through our words, actions, or even silence?
5. What would it look like for our faith and teaching to reflect the beauty of Christ without wounding the most vulnerable in our pews?

_____
_____
_____
_____
_____
_____
_____
_____
_____
_____
_____

Warm-up Activity: Story Reflection and Group Discussion

Participants will read a true story from an African American woman who is a survivor of IPV in a Pentecostal ministry context. Then, participants will write down and share with the group why they believe the survivor did not receive the help or resources she was seeking from her pastor to leave the abusive marriage.

Resist Retraumatization

Survivor Story

An African American young lady who attended a church in the city experienced early childhood trauma. Now an adult, she was active in children's ministry and the junior missionary board. She met her husband in the church, and the pastor officiated the marriage ceremony. She suffered physical, emotional, and spiritual abuse within the marriage. The church doctrine held a stance against divorce. She petitioned the pastor for marriage counseling; he corrected the husband with words of wisdom and prayed for them. She approached the pastor again without her husband and shared that her husband continued to beat her. The pastor recommended she "go home and pray." No resources were made available to her, nor were any interventions. The abused woman continued to attend church; she was seen sitting in the pews but had no voice, silenced with a holy hush. Despair and disillusionment enveloped her mind, a broken vessel—a life of trauma at home and even at the hands of the church, where God dwells.

Discussion Questions

1. Why do you think the survivor did not receive the support or resources she needed from her pastor or church community?

2. How might church teachings on marriage, divorce, and gender roles have influenced the pastor's response?

3. What message did the woman likely receive both directly and indirectly from the church about her safety and worth?

4. Have you ever had someone disclose abuse to you in a ministry setting? How was it handled and, looking back, would you respond differently today?

_____
_____
_____

This reflection is meant to ground our discussion in lived experience. As you consider your role as a faith leader, think about what kind of fruit your ministry bears when it comes to responding to violence and protecting the vulnerable.

Module 2—Content

Intersectionality: The Road where IPV, Gender, Race, Religion, and Patriarchy Meet

The intersectionality theory, developed by Kimberlé Crenshaw in 1989, is a powerful tool for understanding social and cultural contexts, particularly in the African American community and among the lived experiences of Black women. This theory considers all marginalized and overlooked identities within society and helps to identify potential risk factors for women victim-survivors of IPV. It is at these intersections of social and cultural identities along the life continuum where social justice issues arise. Thus, the tool gives us a way to identify systemic oppression, discrimination, and violence directed toward women, empowering us to address these issues head-on in the Pentecostal church.

For an example of intersectionality of IPV for African American women, see the diagram below:

RESIST RETRAUMATIZATION

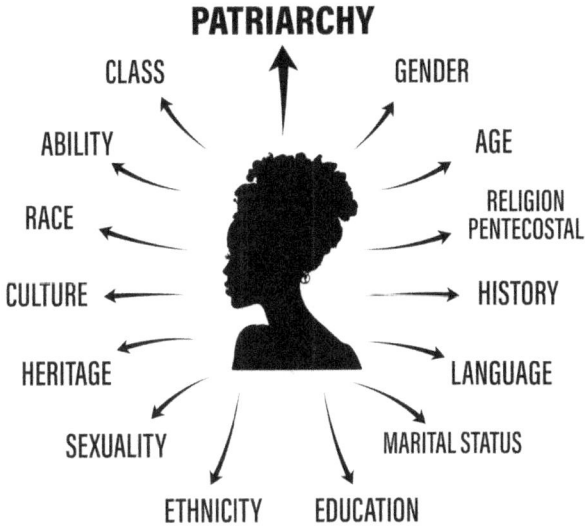

Figure 28. Intersectionality of IPV for African American Women

What Is A Patriarchal Society?

Patriarchal societies influence IPV. This social system is a male-dominated society, wherein men wield predominant power and occupy prominent positions in all spheres of society and domestic life. Most of us grew up within patriarchy. It's built into our families, our churches, our communities. In some ways, it was meant to be a reflection, a way of modeling the authority, care, and strength of Abba Father, our God in heaven. But somewhere along the way, that reflection got distorted.

God is a good Father. He provides, he protects, and he keeps his promises. That's who he is. And in trying to live that out, people built systems where men were given power and responsibility. However, because we live in a fallen world and because we all bear the weight of sin, what was meant to mirror God's heart often becomes something harmful.

Patriarchy, when shaped by sin and not the Spirit, can silence voices that need to be heard. Far too often, the reputations of those in power are protected, while the wounded are left unseen and unheard. As shepherds, we, as church leaders, are called to care for the hurting, not to shield the systems or people that caused their pain. Patriarchy can uphold power instead of offering love. For many women, especially African American women in the church, this has meant being overlooked, dismissed, or asked to carry burdens God never intended.

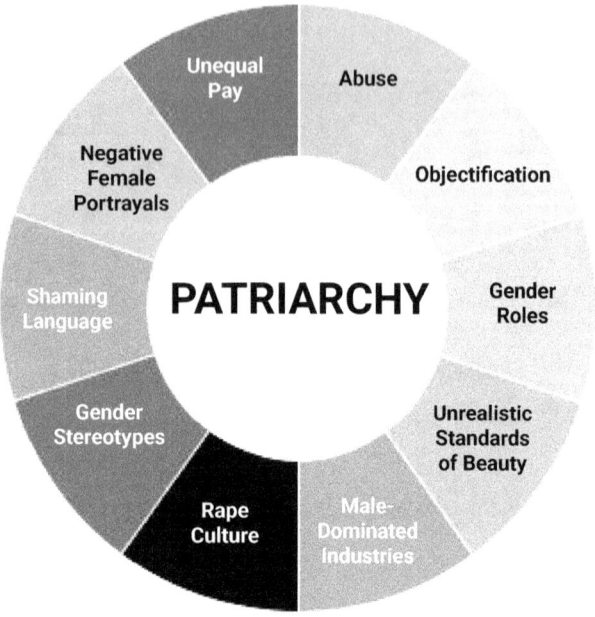

Figure 29. Patriarchy

But here's what we must hold on to: God never intended for one to dominate the other. he made both man and woman in his image to reflect his goodness together. God doesn't play favorites. He doesn't assign worth based on gender. He calls all of us sons and daughters to walk in truth, compassion, and justice.

So, if we truly want to reflect Abba, our Father, then we have to ask hard questions. We need to examine how our churches and traditions may have misinterpreted the concept of headship. God's version of leadership always looks like love, and his power always moves through grace.

We have to be honest about something: patriarchy isn't just "out there" in the world. It also appears in our churches. It shapes how we talk about leadership, submission, family, and even what it means to be a godly woman or man. In many Pentecostal spaces, these beliefs are passed down with good intentions, but they can also become harmful when they silence victims or protect their image over safety.

For African American women, the weight is even heavier. Many are taught to honor their husbands, protect Black men from the injustices of the world, and stay strong for the sake of the family. Add in church teachings that discourage divorce and elevate male headship, and you can see how a woman might feel trapped, with nowhere to tell the truth.

This isn't just about individual behavior. It's about systems: racism that makes Black women less likely to be believed or supported; sexism that says women should stay silent; and religious traditions that, at times, prioritize male authority over women's safety. Consequently, examining Pentecostal ministry environments necessitates analyzing the patriarchal culture that influences social norms in intimate partner relationships.

We're not here to condemn the church. We're here because we love the church. However, if we want our churches to be sanctuaries, we must look honestly at the kind of culture we've created and be willing to change what is hurting people.

Discussion Questions

1. Where have you seen patriarchy or misapplied theology impact how abuse is handled in your church or denomination?

2. How might cultural expectations around gender and race affect whether a Black woman feels safe disclosing IPV in a church setting?

3. What teachings or traditions in your ministry need to be reexamined to ensure that they aren't causing more harm than good?

4. What can clergy and church leaders do differently to help African American women feel seen, believed, and supported when they are experiencing abuse?

Breaking the Silence: Three Pentecostal Challenges that Can Keep Clergy from Seeing and Supporting Survivors of IPV

As clergy and faith leaders, we are called to examine how our theology and traditions either liberate or burden the people we serve, especially those who have experienced trauma. Within Pentecostal spaces, specific theological frameworks and institutional practices can unintentionally reinforce systems of inequality and silence the very voices Jesus came to uplift. Three areas show up often in Pentecostal spaces that prevent clergy from realizing, recognizing, and responding to IPV, unintentionally retraumatizing victim-survivors instead:

- Institutional Pentecostalism—how we structure leadership
- Pentecostal Hermeneutics—how we read the Bible
- Pentecostal Theology—how we talk about God's nature

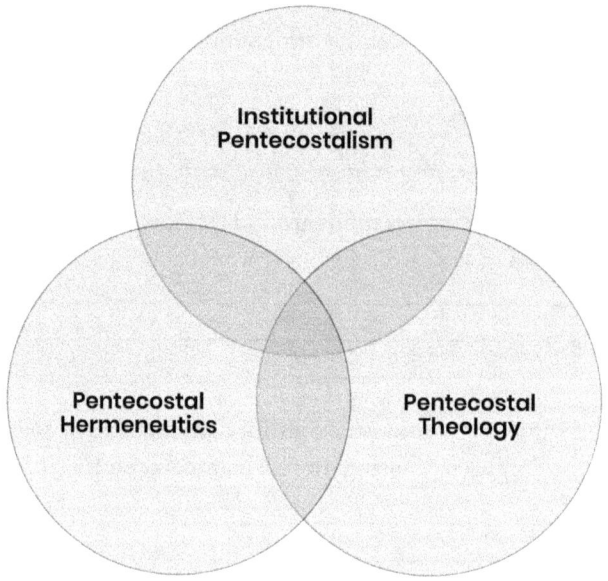

Figure 30. Intersectionality of Pentecostal Risk Factors for IPV

When left unexamined, each of these potential risk factors can unintentionally contribute to silencing survivors of violence and reinforcing inequality, especially for African American women who are deeply committed to their faith but often unheard in church leadership. The more the three Pentecostal risks intersect, the greater the risk factor for enabling IPV.

The facilitator will guide an inclusive dialogue around each risk factor. Participants will engage in "Open Dialogue No Debate" regarding the risk factors to inform the ministry context.

Institutional Pentecostalism

This is the way Pentecostal churches are organized, with respect to who holds power, who gets to lead, and who gets to speak. In many spaces, this structure reflects male-dominated patterns, where men are seen as the spiritual leaders and women as their supporters. While this may have been built with good intentions, it can shut out the voices of women who are called, are gifted, and carry profound wisdom, especially in communities where women already do much of the emotional and spiritual labor.

Transformative Conversations

- Are there women in our church who are gifted to lead but aren't given the chance?
- How might our structures reflect culture more than Christ?

Notes: _____

_____
_____
_____
_____
_____
_____
_____
_____
_____
_____
_____
_____
_____
_____
_____
_____

Pentecostal Hermeneutics

In our tradition, we take the Bible seriously. We trust the Spirit to speak through Scripture. However, sometimes, that trust can lead us to read the Bible in a way that overlooks historical context or silences genuine pain. When someone says, "Wives, submit to your husbands," without understanding what that meant in the ancient world or what it sounds like to someone being abused, it can do real damage. It can keep people trapped in cycles of silence and shame.

Transformative Conversations

- How do we interpret Scripture in ways that uphold justice, not just order?
- Have we ever used the Bible in ways that unintentionally harmed someone?

Notes: _____

_____
_____
_____
_____
_____
_____
_____
_____
_____
_____
_____
_____
_____
_____
_____
_____
_____
_____
_____

Pentecostal Theology

We talk about God as Father, Son, and Holy Spirit. Sometimes, churches use this language to shape family roles: God the Father (authority), Jesus the Son (obedient), and the Spirit (helper). Then, we assign these roles to men, women, and children. But the Trinity is not a power structure; it's a relationship. It's unity, equality, and love working together. When we turn it into a chain of command, we miss the beauty of God's relational nature and use his name to justify inequality.

Transformative Conversations

- How has Trinitarian theology shaped our view of leadership and family roles?
- What would it look like to model ministry after mutuality rather than hierarchy?

Notes: _____
_____
_____
_____
_____
_____
_____
_____
_____
_____
_____
_____
_____
_____
_____
_____

God didn't call us to guard power. He called us to shepherd people. That means being willing to revisit long-held assumptions and ask, "Is this producing freedom, or is it reinforcing fear?" Abuse, whether physical, emotional, or spiritual, should never have a place in God's house. But it's there. And if we don't name it, we can't heal it.

This work takes humility. It takes courage. But more than anything, it takes love, the kind of love that listens, that changes, that lifts people out of silence and shame and tells them, "You matter. You are seen. You are safe here."

Exit Ticket

Three things you found important.
_____
_____
_____

Two things that change your thinking.
_____
_____
_____

One thing you want to learn more about.
_____
_____
_____

Action Step: Clergy Safety Resource Assignment: Preparing to Respond with Wisdom

Each participant will take time to create or locate an up-to-date list of local resources for survivors of IPV, including women's shelters, crisis hotlines, counseling services, and advocacy organizations in your area.

This list should be completed within 30 days of completing this training and kept in a location that is easily accessible in case someone discloses abuse and requests help.

Please note that we do not distribute this list unless the woman explicitly requests support or safety options. Offering unsolicited resources can feel unsafe or overwhelming. Instead, we practice listening, honoring her pace, and being ready to respond with care when she is prepared to receive help.

This is one small but powerful way we create safety and dignity for those who may be suffering in silence.

Personal Journal of Reflection and Prayer

This journal space is an invitation to pause, reflect, and connect with yourself, with God, and with the truths that have emerged during this training. As you write, allow your thoughts, emotions, and prayers to flow freely. There is no right or wrong way to reflect; this is your sacred space for honest dialogue with your soul and your Creator.

You may consider journaling about the following:

- What stirred your spirit during today's session?
- How is God speaking to you about your role in healing and advocacy?
- What past experiences of harm, silence, hope, or strength are surfacing?
- What prayers do you need to pray for yourself, for survivors, or for your community?

Take this time to be gentle with yourself. Let your pen become a voice of release, discovery, and prayerful commitment. Remember, healing is a journey, and reflection is a decisive step forward.

_____
_____
_____
_____
_____
_____
_____
_____
_____
_____
_____
_____
_____
_____
_____
_____
_____
_____

MODULE THREE

Respond

Module 3: Respond (Day 3)

This module empowers you to **respond** with practical tools, pastoral care strategies, and biblical wisdom that reflect God's justice and mercy. You will explore how to create safe, supportive spaces for survivors, preach and teach with sensitivity, and build collaborative networks of care. Here, responding becomes an act of worship embodying the hands and heart of Christ.

By the end of this module, you will:

- Acquire the fundamental principles of trauma-informed care, which serve as the framework for trauma-informed theology, as this understanding is crucial for the rest of the module's learning outcomes.
- Recognize the profound and lasting effects of historical trauma on the lived experiences of African Americans, especially within faith communities.

Reflect on and assess your cultural awareness and sensitivity, particularly toward African American women across the lifespan, as this is a key aspect of providing effective support.

Focus Activity

Movement 3—Making the Story Our Own: Connecting biblical healing to communal transformation

Opening Prayer

Righteous and Sovereign God, we come before You in the mighty name of Jesus, confessing that we have not always been faithful stewards of the souls You've placed under our care. We repent for the times we have ignored the cries of those suffering from trauma and intimate partner violence. We have too often spiritualized suffering rather than confronting injustice.

We have preached healing without creating space for the broken to be seen. Forgive us, Lord, for staying silent when You called us to speak. For remaining still when You stirred us to act. You are the God of justice; true and righteous are Your judgments. Teach us to be shepherds who do not wound but protect. Make us ministers of your healing presence to those who are physically, emotionally, and spiritually injured.

Baptize us anew with Pentecostal fire, not only to prophesy and preach but to listen with compassion, to discern with wisdom, and to respond with courage. Empower us to build communities of refuge where silence is broken, shame is dismantled, and survivors are believed, seen, and restored. May our pulpits never be louder than our compassion. May our theology never override our responsibility. And may our ministry reflect Your heart for justice.

We surrender ourselves to this holy work. In Jesus' mighty and merciful name, we pray,

Amen.

Icebreaker

Participants share what the Bible verse and African proverb for Module 3 means to them.

Scripture

> I heard the altar **respond**: "Yes, Lord God Almighty, true and just are your judgments."—Rev 16:7

What does this Bible verse mean to me?

In this verse, we witness something profound: the altar speaks. This isn't just symbolic; it's sacred. The altar, that place of sacrifice, worship, and divine encounter, becomes a voice affirming what we need to remember in the face of deep suffering: God's justice is real, and it is right.

For those of us serving in Pentecostal ministry as pastors, caregivers, and spiritual leaders, this verse calls us to pause and reflect. Are we reflecting that same justice in how we respond to trauma and intimate partner violence? Are we listening to the cries that rise from the broken places, cries that God hears even when we don't?

Rev 16:7 reminds us that suffering does not go unnoticed by God. Divine justice leans in close. And if God hears and responds, then we, too, must become voices at the altar echoing his justice, advocating for healing, and standing with those who've been wounded.

1. What does it mean to affirm that God's judgments are true and just in the face of abuse or injustice?

2. How does this verse challenge or affirm the way I minister to those wounded by IPV?

3. In what ways can my preaching, pastoring, or leadership reflect God's heart for justice and healing?

4. How can the church become an "altar" that speaks on behalf of the wounded?

___

African Proverb

"Three things cause sorrow to flee: water, green trees, and a beautiful face."—Moroccan proverb

What is the meaning of this African proverb?

There's profound wisdom here. This African proverb reminds us that sometimes, the most potent healing doesn't come through words but through presence. Through creation. Through beauty. Through something, someone that helps us remember we're still alive.

In the context of trauma and IPV, this saying speaks volumes. It reminds us that healing isn't always loud. Sometimes, it starts in quiet spaces in the safety of a room, in the shade of something steady, or in the kindness of a face that sees you and doesn't look away.

As Pentecostal ministers, we've been shaped to expect healing in the shout, at the altar, in the fire. And yes, God meets us there. But this proverb gently reminds us that God also heals in the hush. In the calm. In the moments that feel like water on dry skin or the steady presence of something deeply rooted. Sometimes healing is a hand held, a soft word, or just being present long enough for the sorrow to breathe and begin to go.

Water cleanses the trees around us. And a beautiful face, the kind that reflects Christ's compassion, can make sorrow start to lose its grip. Survivors don't just need theology; they need us. They need our presence to feel like living water, like rooted trees, like faces that say with no pretense, *"You are safe here."*

1. In your ministry setting, what might "water" symbolize for someone who is navigating trauma or IPV?
2. Green trees suggest life, rootedness, and growth. How can we as leaders become rooted enough to provide consistent, safe, and stable support for those who are hurting?
3. The phrase "a beautiful face" may suggest the power of kindness, gentleness, and non-judgmental presence.
4. This proverb implies that sorrow can begin to loosen its grip in the presence of safety and beauty.

_____
_____
_____
_____
_____
_____
_____
_____

Warm-up Activity

To help participants embody what it means to be a healing presence like water, rooted trees, and a kind face when ministering to survivors of trauma or IPV.

Part 1: Reflection Circle (10 minutes)

Instructions:
    Invite participants to sit in a circle or small groups. Read the revised proverb and reflect aloud (or have a participant volunteer to read it). Then, ask each person to respond to this prompt:
    "Think of a time when someone's presence, not their words, helped ease your sorrow. What did that feel like? What did they do or not do?"
    (Allow 1–2 people per group to share. Keep this reflective, not overly detailed. Remind them to hold each other's stories gently.)

Part 2: Role Play—"Water, Tree, Face" (15-20 minutes)

Setup:

Participants will break into groups of three. Each person will rotate through one of the following roles:

1. **The Survivor:** A person sitting in silence, carrying a heavy emotional burden (trauma or IPV, no graphic detail needed).
2. **The Minister:** A clergy member practicing what it means to be a healing presence (water, rooted tree, or kind face).
3. **The Observer:** Watches and provides gentle feedback using the following question:

    "Did the minister's presence reflect safety, rootedness, or compassion?"

Scenario:

The "survivor" does not want to talk about what happened. The minister is not there to offer solutions, Scripture, or prayers but rather just presence.

They are challenged to embody one of the following:

Water: Calm, gentle, soothing.

Tree: Grounded, non-anxious, steady.

Face: Attentive, kind, affirming.

Time: 3–4 minutes per round. Rotate roles until everyone has been in each role once.

Debrief (10 minutes)

As a whole group, discuss:

What did it feel like to be present and not fix?

_____
_____
_____

Which presence of water, tree, or face felt most natural to you?

_____

How might this exercise change how you engage someone in your congregation who is living with trauma or IPV?

Module 3—Content

What Is Trauma?

Trauma occurs when an event or situation overwhelms a person's ability to cope emotionally, physically, or spiritually. It can come from a single devastating event, like an assault, a serious accident, or a natural disaster. But it can also come from repeated exposure to harm, like abuse, neglect, or living in constant fear.

In the immediate aftermath, people often feel numb or in shock; it's the body and mind's way of trying to protect itself. But as time passes, the effects of trauma can show up in many ways: sudden emotional outbursts, feeling disconnected or "not like yourself," trouble sleeping, headaches, or even withdrawing from loved ones.

These responses aren't signs of weakness or a lack of faith. They're signs that the nervous system is still trying to make sense of something too big, too painful, or too fast. While many people eventually find their way forward, some get stuck in the pain. And that's where the church can and must be part of their healing, not another layer of hurt.

What Is Trauma-Informed Care?

As pastors and spiritual leaders, our role in trauma-informed care is crucial. Many of us have prayed with people whose stories hold more than just surface-level pain. We've seen the tears that don't fall, the silence that speaks louder than words, and the smiles that mask deep wounds. To walk faithfully with God's people—especially those impacted by trauma and intimate partner violence—we must understand that trauma is often present, even when it isn't named.

Trauma-informed care is more than a strategy; it's a ministry posture. It helps us as leaders realize just how common trauma is and invites us to create a culture of safety, healing, and dignity in everything we do.

This approach is often described through a simple but powerful framework known as the 4 Rs.

1. **Realize** the widespread impact of trauma not just in the world but in our congregations, our families, and even in ourselves.
2. **Recognize** the signs of trauma in those we serve not only through behavior but also through body language, emotional reactions, and spiritual distress.
3. **Respond** with compassion and wisdom, shaping our preaching, our counseling, and our leadership in ways that reflect Christ's care for the wounded.
4. **Resist** retraumatization by building environments where people feel seen, safe, and supported, not shamed or silenced.

This framework equips us with the tools to navigate the complexities of trauma in our ministry, empowering us to serve with compassion and wisdom.

Being trauma-informed doesn't mean we become therapists. It means we become more like Jesus, the One who never ignored the pain, never rushed healing, and never turned away the broken.

In a Pentecostal context, this care is closely tied to our belief in the power of the Holy Spirit. The same Spirit who gives us boldness also calls us to gentleness. And sometimes, the most Spirit-filled thing we can do is to slow down, listen deeply, and hold space for the healing God is already doing, knowing that the Holy Spirit is guiding us every step of the way.

Six core principles guide trauma-informed care.[33] They help us examine how we preach, counsel, lead, and love in ways that reflect the heart of Jesus, the Great Healer:

Safety

People can't begin to heal if they don't feel safe. Our churches, pulpits, and prayer lines must become spaces where minds, bodies, and spirits are protected—not just from harm but from shame.

---

33. Wilson, et al., "Trauma-Informed Care."

Trauma-Informed Theology

Trustworthiness and Transparency

Trust is earned when we show up consistently and communicate clearly. Being trauma-informed means we don't manipulate emotions, overpromise healing, or spiritualize someone's suffering. We walk with them in honesty and grace.

Peer Support

Healing often begins when someone hears, *"You're not alone."* The church can be a place of shared testimony, where survivors connect, encourage one another, and hold space for each other. Peer support reminds us of the power of community to carry burdens together.

Collaboration and Mutuality

This is not about hierarchy. We are not above the people we serve. Trauma-informed ministry honors the humanity of each person. We listen as much as we lead, and we recognize the Holy Spirit speaks through the people, too.

Empowerment, Voice, and Choice

Trauma often robs people of their voice. Our job is not to speak over them but to help them reclaim it. We create opportunities for survivors to make choices, to be heard, and to grow in the freedom Christ offers.

Cultural, Historical, and Gender Awareness

We cannot genuinely care for people if we ignore their origins. Historical trauma, systemic racism, and gender-based violence are real forces that shape how people experience life and faith. Trauma-informed care means we honor that complexity with humility and compassion.

To be trauma-informed as Pentecostal clergy is not to abandon power. It's to wield it as Jesus did: with gentleness, truth, and healing. The Holy Ghost doesn't just fall in the shout. Sometimes, the Spirit whispers through safety, through presence, through deep listening and quiet trust.

Notes: _____
_____
_____
_____
_____
_____
_____
_____
_____
_____
_____
_____
_____
_____
_____
_____
_____
_____
_____
_____
_____
_____
_____
_____
_____
_____

What Is Trauma-Informed Theology?

Trauma-informed theology begins where human suffering begins in Gen 3:15. This is where the story shifts. Brokenness enters the world and, with it, the reality of conflict, pain, and disconnection. From that moment on, the biblical narrative becomes not just a story of faith but a story of trauma and healing.

In ministry, especially within Pentecostal spaces, we must hold this tension with care. Trauma-informed theology weaves together the principles of trauma-informed care—Realize, Recognize, Respond, and Resist Retraumatization—with our spiritual, liturgical, and pastoral practices. It's a way of ministering that seeks to *do no further harm* to those who have already carried more than their share of suffering.

This framework invites us to read Scripture not as a distant record but as a living witness to suffering and survival, a powerful tool for transformation. Trauma is not a modern disruption. It is part of the human story, and the Bible does not shy away from it. We hear it in Sarah's cries, see it in Tamar's silence, feel it in Joseph's betrayal, and mourn with David in his grief. We walk with Ruth through uncertainty, sit with Elijah in his despair, and stand at the cross with Jesus in his suffering. These are not just sacred stories of the past. They are holy mirrors. For so many in our congregations, these wounds are not symbolic; they are lived. And when we name that truth from the pulpit, we create space for healing to begin.

Trauma-informed theology helps us recognize that the gospel isn't just good news for the strong and victorious; it's also for the wounded, the weary, and the survivors. It challenges us to interpret Scripture in ways that make space for lament, resilience, and restoration.

As Pentecostal clergy, we believe in the power of healing. Trauma-informed theology doesn't weaken our witness; it strengthens it. It deepens it. It calls us to preach and minister in ways that are both Spirit-filled and tender, prophetic and protective. It teaches us that true healing isn't just in the altar call. It's in how we make space for stories, hold silence with reverence, and treat the broken with honor.

Grounding Activities

To help clergy explore how trauma shows up in the biblical narrative, reflect on their theological lens, and consider how to minister with both spiritual authority and emotional sensitivity.

Part 1: Read and Lament

1. **Scripture Meditation**

Slowly read Gen 3:15 aloud. Sit with the tension in this verse and how pain enters the human story.

What stands out to you? What emotions are stirred as you consider this as a beginning point for trauma?

2. **Personal Lament**

Take a few minutes to journal your response to this prompt:

Lord, what have I overlooked in the stories of pain in Scripture or in the lives of those I serve?

3. Write a short prayer of lament or confession.

Part 2: Trauma in the Sacred Text

Choose one biblical figure from this list:

Sarah, Tamar, Ruth, David, Elijah, Joseph, Paul, Jesus.

Answer these prompts in writing or small group discussion:

- What trauma or loss did this person experience?
- How did God meet them in their pain?
- What parallels do you see in the lives of people you minister to?
- How might your preaching or pastoral care reflect their story more compassionately?

Part 3: Ministry Self-Reflection

Reflect personally or in quiet prayer:

- Have I ever unintentionally caused harm by spiritualizing someone's pain too quickly?
- In what ways can I create space in my ministry for people's trauma to be acknowledged without judgment?
- What would it mean for me to become a *trauma-informed preacher*? A *trauma-informed intercessor*?

Why Is Cultural Competency Critical in Pentecostal Ministry?

When we widen our lens on trauma, we move beyond the personal and into the generational and historical stories that shape entire communities. This is essential for developing true cultural competency in ministry. It means paying attention to the ways trauma shows up differently depending on one's cultural background, lineage, and lived experience. For African American women, especially those impacted by IPV, trauma is often compounded by the weight of history that has been passed down through generations of struggle, survival, and silence. Understanding this layered reality enables us to minister more truthfully, with empathy rooted in context rather than just compassion. It invites us to listen differently, respond more thoughtfully, and hold space for the whole story, not just the surface pain.

What Is Historical Trauma?

Historical trauma is the deep wound carried across generations by communities who have experienced systemic violence, oppression, or displacement. It's not just about one moment in time. It's the ongoing impact of events like slavery, genocide, forced migration, and colonization that targeted people because of their race, culture, or identity.

This kind of trauma doesn't fade with time. It is passed down not only through stories or silence but also through the body, the mind, and the soul—generational trauma and post-traumatic slave syndrome. People may carry fear, mistrust, or grief they can't fully explain. Families and communities may struggle with cycles of pain that have roots in injustice far beyond their lifetime.

For those of us called to ministry, recognizing historical trauma invites a shift in both posture and perspective. We move away from asking, "What's wrong with them?" and instead lean in with compassion to ask, "What happened to their ancestors? What story is their family carrying and how might we become part of their healing?" It's a sacred call to tend not only to personal pain but also to generational wounds, honoring the holy work of restoration, repair, and remembrance.

Developing Cultural Competency in Spirit-Filled Ministry

In trauma-informed, Spirit-led ministry, cultural competency isn't optional. It's sacred work. It is how we create spaces where people from all walks of life feel seen, heard, and valued. Cultural competency helps us communicate with care, minister with understanding, and preach a gospel that reflects God's heart for every nation, tribe, and tongue.

RESIST RETRAUMATIZATION

One helpful guide is Cross's Six Stages of Cultural Competence,[34] which outlines the development of individuals and institutions over time. These stages include:

1. **Cultural Destructiveness**—This is when systems, policies, or attitudes do direct harm to people from different cultural backgrounds. It's more than ignorance. It's when culture is devalued, disrespected, or outright attacked, often in ways woven into the very fabric of an organization.

   Question:

   In what ways have church systems knowingly or unknowingly participated in practices that harmed or excluded people from different cultural backgrounds? How might we begin to name and repair that harm?

   _____
   _____
   _____

2. **Cultural Incapacity**—This occurs when there is a lack of readiness or even resistance to engaging with people from diverse cultural backgrounds. It's not always intentional, but the impact is the same and often goes unmet. People feel invisible, and harm continues because we're not prepared to respond with understanding.

   Question:

   Are there people in our congregation or community whose needs we consistently overlook because we lack the understanding or ability to respond to their unique cultural experiences? What are we willing to do to change that?

   _____
   _____
   _____

3. **Cultural Blindness**—This is the "we're all the same" mindset. While it may sound appealing on the surface, it overlooks the profound differences in people's lived experiences, access to resources, and historical realities. When we pretend not to see culture, we also fail to see the inequities tied to it.

---

34. Cross et al., "A Monograph on Effective Services for Minority Children," 1–90.

Question:

Have we ever said or believed "we're all the same" in a way that dismissed someone's lived experience? What would it look like to honor both our shared humanity and our cultural differences in ministry?

_____
_____
_____

4. **Cultural Pre-Competence**—This is the moment we start to wake up. We recognize our blind spots. We realize we've got work to do. And we begin seeking out growth, not just to appear culturally aware, but because we care about doing better for real people in real pain.

Question:

What are we starting to notice about our limitations when it comes to cultural awareness? Where do we feel a holy discomfort, and how might the Holy Spirit be inviting us to grow?

_____
_____
_____

5. **Cultural Competence**—At this stage, we actively practice inclusion, learn how to listen across differences, and build environments where diversity is welcomed and respected. It's not a checkbox. It's a rhythm we commit to.

Question:

How are we actively practicing respect, inclusion, and cultural responsiveness in our preaching, leadership, and pastoral care? What are the fruits— and where is God calling us deeper?

_____
_____
_____

6. **Cultural Proficiency**—Here, culture isn't something extra we add on—it becomes core to how we lead, serve, and make decisions. It shapes our theology, our policies, and our ministry practices. It's where equity becomes part of the ministry's DNA.

Question:

Is cultural awareness truly woven into the heart of our ministry, or is it still something we "add on"? How can we move from occasional inclusion to Spirit-led transformation that reflects God's justice and love for all people?

_____

_____

_____

Let's be clear: cultural competence isn't about trying to become an expert on someone else's culture. It's not about carrying guilt, performing allyship to look good, or borrowing pieces of someone's identity we haven't taken the time to understand. At its core, it's about presence. It's about showing up with humility, listening with care, and honoring the image of God in every person. It's about making room for healing and justice to take root in the spaces we lead.

For those of us called to Pentecostal ministry, this work is deeply spiritual. It's a posture of humility and a commitment to telling the truth. As we welcome the fire of the Holy Spirit, we must also welcome the refining fire that challenges bias, dismantles silence, and calls us to be bridges, especially for those whose cultures have long been ignored, wounded, or erased.

Group Activity: Mapping the Wounds and Witness—A Timeline of African American Historical Trauma

Participants will work together in small groups to create a visual timeline that highlights significant moments in African American history that have contributed to generational and community trauma. Encourage them to consider both pain and perseverance—moments that caused deep harm and moments where God's sustaining presence and the community's resilience were evident.

Instructions:

1. Begin with the transatlantic slave trade and move forward through significant historical periods (e.g., slavery, Reconstruction, Jim Crow, Civil Rights Movement, mass incarceration, modern-day racial violence).

Trauma-Informed Theology

2. Include events that have had a spiritual, social, or emotional impact on African American communities.
3. Use symbols, drawings, or Scripture verses that speak to both the trauma and the faith that carried people through it.
4. After creating the timeline, have each group briefly share what they noticed, learned, or felt during the process.

Notes: _____

This activity deepens awareness of the legacy of historical trauma, particularly in the lives of African American congregants today, and helps clergy develop a more compassionate and informed pastoral response rooted in cultural and spiritual sensitivity.

The African American Experience of Trauma through the Expression of Adinkra Symbols

The word *Adinkra* comes from the Twi language spoken by the Asante people of Ghana. Traditionally, it's a farewell, something said when parting ways. But it's more than just "goodbye." It's a message, a symbol, a reflection of meaning carried between souls.

Adinkra symbols are deeply rooted in West African culture, with their significance spanning generations and continents. Nearly half of the Africans enslaved and brought to the United States came from West Africa. In fact, during the height of the transatlantic slave trade, one in every six enslaved West Africans went from this very region. These symbols, carved into textiles, pottery, and metalwork, weren't just decorative; they denoted language, resistance, and memory.

Adinkra symbols carry wisdom, identity, and truth that help us name and confront the layers of trauma passed down through generations. For African American women, especially those who have survived IPV, this history matters. These symbols are not just art. They are sacred echoes calling us to recognize pain, honor survival, and lean into the work of healing.

For us, as Pentecostal clergy engaging with this curriculum, these symbols are not only culturally important but also spiritually significant. They reconnect us to the African origins of the African American community and remind us of the beauty and resilience embedded in the diaspora.

But they also invite us to face what must be healed.

The African Adinkra symbols' names and meanings follow:

Gye Nyame, meaning "except for God," symbolizes God's omnipotence through the knowledge that people should not fear anything except God.[35]

---

35. National Park Service, "Gye Nyame—Supremacy of God."

Figure 31. "Gye Nyamme" African Adinkra Symbol

Nsoromma, which translates to "children of the heavens" or "star," serves as a symbol representing the divine guardianship of God and his omnipresent watchfulness over all living entities.[36]

Figure 32. "Nsoromma," African Adinkra Symbol

Matie Masie means "what I hear, I keep." The emblem of four linked ears reminds individuals to listen and communicate, especially in oral cultures. It represents wisdom and knowledge through sound judgment and insight.[37]

---

36. National Park Service, "Nsoromma—Guardianship."
37. National Park Service, "Matie Masie"—Wisdom and Prudence."

Figure 33. "Matie Masie," African Adinkra Symbol

Akoma ntoso means "linked hearts." The emblem symbolizes four hearts intertwined, representing soul immortality and sympathy. Akoma ntoso also unites families and communities.[38]

Figure 34. "Akoma Ntoso," African Adinkra Symbol

Denkyem means "crocodile." This Adinkra symbol represents adaptability because the crocodile can breathe underwater despite living in swamps and water. During the Transatlantic slave trade, enslaved Africans were taken from their homes in Africa and put in a place they did not know. This symbol represents all Africans in the diaspora.[39]

---

38. National Park Service, "Akoma Ntoso—Understanding."
39. National Park Service, "Denkyem—Adaptability."

Figure 35. "Denkyem," African Adinkra Symbol

Sankofa is a communication technique and a symbol. The symbol's iconography communicates the phrase "Look to the past to guide the future," which can be interpreted as drawing insights and lessons from historical events and experiences to influence future actions and decisions.[40] Slavery is a painful but central part of the African American narrative, and acknowledging its legacy is imperative for societal healing and progress.

Figure 36. "Sankofa," African Adinkra Symbol

---

40. National Park Service, "Sankofa—Learn from the Past."

Transformative Conversations

1. **Adinkra as Farewell and Memory**

   How does the idea of "farewell" take on new meaning when we think about the forced departure of African people through slavery? In what ways do symbols like Adinkra reconnect us to stories that were never meant to be forgotten?

   _____
   _____
   _____

2. **Spiritual Significance of Cultural Memory**

   What role does cultural memory play in spiritual healing? How can we, as Pentecostal clergy, honor the sacred stories embedded in the African diaspora within our preaching, pastoral care, and community work?

   _____
   _____
   _____

3. **Generational and Interpersonal Trauma**

   In what ways do you see the impact of historical and generational trauma show up in the lives of African American women especially survivors of IPV in your congregation or community?

   _____
   _____
   _____

4. **Symbols as Tools for Healing**

   How might Adinkra symbols serve as visual reminders of both the wounds and the resilience of a people in their theology? Could they help foster healing spaces in your ministry? If so, how?

   _____
   _____
   _____

5. **Pentecostal Ministry and Cultural Integration**

   How can our Spirit-filled traditions better embrace cultural identity and ancestral wisdom without compromising biblical integrity? What might it look like to include these elements in worship, teaching, or pastoral counseling?

   _____
   _____
   _____

6. **Responsibility to the Past, Commitment to the Future**

   As clergy, how are we called to confront systems and spiritual narratives that have dismissed or erased Black pain and resilience? What does it mean to be a prophetic witness who helps people grieve and heal collectively?

   _____
   _____
   _____

Exit Ticket

Three things you found important.

_____
_____
_____

Two things that change your thinking.

_____
_____
_____

One thing you want to learn more about.

_____
_____
_____

Action Step: Clergy Response Plan: Walking with Those Who Disclose Abuse

The participants will draft a response plan for clergy when someone discloses abuse. Participants will invite a local social worker or trauma counselor to lead a Q&A for their auxiliary ministries before the end of the year.

As part of our commitment to care well for those we serve, each participant will take time to prayerfully draft a simple, compassionate response plan for what to do when someone comes forward and shares that they've experienced abuse. This plan doesn't need to be perfect. It just needs to reflect on your heart to protect, listen, and act wisely. Think about what you would do at that moment to ensure safety, honor their voice, and connect them to support without causing more harm.

Next Step: Extending the Conversation in the Community

Before the year ends, each participant will reach out and invite a local trauma counselor, social worker, or advocate to speak with your ministry teams, especially those leading your auxiliaries.

Host a Q&A or open conversation to help them better understand how to respond when someone says, "This happened to me."

This isn't just a training. It's about preparing the people of God to be safe, healing spaces. Because when someone discloses abuse, our response matters. It could be the moment that helps them feel seen or the moment that sends them back into silence. Let's be ready with compassion, clarity, and care.

Personal Journal of Reflection and Prayer

This journal space is an invitation to pause, reflect, and connect with yourself, with God, and with the truths that have emerged during this training. As you write, allow your thoughts, emotions, and prayers to flow freely. There is no right or wrong way to reflect; this is your sacred space for honest dialogue with your soul and your Creator.

You may consider journaling about the following:

- What stirred your spirit during today's session?
- How is God speaking to you about your role in healing and advocacy?
- What past experiences of harm, silence, hope, or strength are surfacing?
- What prayers do you need to pray for yourself, for survivors, or for your community?

Take this time to be gentle with yourself. Let your pen become a voice of release, discovery, and prayerful commitment. Remember, healing is a journey, and reflection is a decisive step forward.

MODULE FOUR

Resist Retraumatization

Module 4: Resist Retraumatization (Day 4)

Finally, we focus on how to **resist retraumatization** within church practices, theology, and leadership. This module addresses harmful patterns, whether in preaching, counseling, or church culture, that may unintentionally cause further harm. Through the guidance of the Holy Spirit, we are called to build communities of restoration where healing is ongoing, and the image of God is honored in all.

By the end of this module, participants will:

- Identify language, practices, and church dynamics that may retraumatize IPV survivors and understand the significant impact of Adverse Childhood Experiences (ACEs) and the essential role of mandated reporting.
- Develop a personal response plan for IPV disclosures and initiate the process of shaping trauma-informed policies for their ministry context.
- Write and deliver a sermon or teaching that applies the 4Rs of trauma-informed care (Realize, Recognize, Respond, and Resist Re-traumatization), gaining confidence in addressing IPV from the pulpit.

Focus Activity

Movement 4—Discernment to Praxis: Creating trauma-informed action and sustaining transformed ministry

Opening Prayer

    Father God,

    We come before You as Your servants and shepherds, humbled by the call to care for Your people. Holy Spirit, awaken our hearts so that we may discern the hidden pain in the pews and recognize where our words, practices, or traditions may be wounding those already scarred by abuse and trauma.

    Give us eyes to see the silent suffering and ears to hear what isn't said aloud. Teach us to walk with wisdom and compassion, not just in power but in tenderness. We ask You, Lord, to anoint us afresh, not only for deliverance and breakthrough but for gentleness, safety, and Spirit-led discernment. Let our altars be places of healing, not harm.

Let our preaching carry the fire of the Holy Ghost but also the balm of Gilead for the brokenhearted. Help us to be mindful stewards of Your Word, preaching not from our strength but from a place of humility and grace. May we never retraumatize those seeking refuge but instead be vessels of Your presence that calms storms and restores souls. Guide us to create sanctuaries where survivors of IPV and trauma are seen, heard, and held.

Let our churches become safe harbors where shame is broken, silence is lifted, and Your healing flows freely. We declare that the Spirit of the Lord is upon us to carry the good news to those who are hurting, to tend gently to the hearts that have been broken, and to proclaim freedom and restoration to all who feel bound by trauma. We accept Your call to do no harm. And we say yes to leading with compassion, truth, and the power of Your Spirit.

In Jesus' Name, Amen.

Icebreaker

Participants share what the Bible verse and African proverb for Module 4 means to them.

Scripture

> Resist him, standing firm in the faith, because you know that the family of believers throughout the world is undergoing the same kind of sufferings. —1 Pet 5:9

What does this Bible verse mean to me?

As ministry leaders, we are often called to stand in the gap for others, especially those who carry deep wounds from trauma, violence, and hardship. This can be exhausting and sacred work. But Scripture reminds us that we do not stand alone. Others across the body of Christ are enduring similar battles. The enemy we resist is real, but so is the power and presence of God that strengthens us.

This verse is both a challenge and a comfort. It calls us to spiritual resistance to hold our ground in faith, and it also assures us that our suffering is not isolated. We are part of a global body, walking through suffering together.

1. How does standing "steadfast in the faith" shape the way we respond to those in our congregations who are silently suffering from trauma or abuse?
2. In what ways can we cultivate spiritual environments where people feel safe to name their suffering without fear, shame, or spiritual dismissal?
3. How does the knowledge that others are experiencing "the same kinds of suffering" invite us into deeper compassion and connection with both our members and fellow leaders?
4. What might spiritual resistance look like when caring for survivors of IPV and generational trauma within the African American community?

_____
_____
_____
_____
_____
_____
_____
_____
_____
_____
_____
_____

African Proverb

> "When sleeping women wake, they move mountains!"
> —African proverb

What is the meaning of this African proverb?

This proverb reminds us of something we've always known deep down—women carry a strength that is spiritual, emotional, and passed down through generations. But far too often, that strength has been buried beneath the weight of trauma. Too many women have been silenced, not just by the world but by the very systems and spaces that were meant to help them heal, including the church.

As Pentecostal leaders, we believe in awakening. We preach revival, renewal, and restoration. But here's the question we must ask ourselves: Are we truly making room for women to rise into the fullness of who God has called them to be? Are our pulpits, pews, and prayer circles places where women feel safe to speak, to heal, and to be believed?

To resist retraumatization is to say: "No more silence. No more shame. No More Holy Hush!" It's a commitment to protect the voices God is awakening. It means showing up for survivors of IPV and trauma, not just with our prayers, but with real, Spirit-led actions. It means breaking down the walls of silence, of misuse, of spiritual control that has kept too many of our sisters sleeping when God is calling them to rise.

1. In what ways has the church unintentionally contributed to the silencing of women's voices, especially those impacted by trauma or IPV, and how can we begin to reverse that?

2. What does it look like in our context to "make room" for women to rise in their full, healed identity? Where is the Spirit calling us to clear space for their awakening?

3. What are some spiritual or cultural "mountains" (e.g., shame, silence, fear, theological misuse) that may need to be moved to support survivors in our congregations?

4. How might our preaching, teaching, and pastoral care shift if we truly centered healing, especially for women who have survived abuse and generational trauma?

_____
_____
_____
_____
_____
_____

Warm-up Activities

Before we start today's session, let's pause and consider how our worship spaces—the images, words, and rituals we use every week—might feel to someone carrying invisible wounds. This reflection invites you to look closely at common liturgical practices and symbols that could unintentionally reopen old wounds for survivors of IPV. You will name a few of these potential triggers and begin imagining what a safer, more Spirit-sensitive ministry space might look like. Remember, this reflection is not about dwelling on the past but about envisioning a future where our ministry space is a beacon of hope and healing.

Activity 1: Listening Between the Lines

Title: *When the Pulpit Speaks, Who Listens with Pain?*

Instructions:

Find a quiet place to sit with your thoughts. Close your eyes and recall a recent worship service where you preached or ministered. Take a few deep breaths and consider the following prompts one at a time:

- What words, phrases, or altar practices did I use that may have been heavy or confusing for someone who's experienced abuse?
- Did anything I said imply that suffering is always part of God's will or that endurance means silence?
- Was there space for someone to feel safe enough to remain unseen if needed, or did we demand a response?

Write down whatever comes to your heart, not to critique but to grow awareness. Let the Holy Spirit gently illuminate what may need care or change.

Notes: _____
_____
_____
_____
_____
_____
_____
_____
_____
_____
_____

Activity 2: Visual Discernment—Seeing Through a Survivor's Eyes

Title: What Does This Symbol Say to the Wounded?

Instructions:

Choose three common sacred symbols or practices in your worship space (e.g., the cross, anointing oil, the pastor's seat, altar cloths, vestments, or specific colors and banners). Sit quietly and look at each one (or visualize them if you're not physically in the sanctuary).

Ask yourself:

- If I were a survivor of IPV, what emotions or memories might this image stir in me?
- Does this symbol feel like an invitation to healing, or does it carry pressure, power, or fear?
- Is there anything I want to adjust, not to remove the symbol but to make space for tenderness?

Write a brief note about each image. This is not about judgment. It's about building a sanctuary where no one has to brace themselves to worship.

Notes: _____

_____
_____
_____
_____
_____
_____
_____
_____
_____
_____

Module 4—Content

What Is an Adverse Childhood Experience?

As pastors and ministry leaders, we are often entrusted with the sacred work of hearing stories, some filled with heartache that stretches far beyond the moment of crisis we're witnessing. This is why understanding Adverse Childhood Experiences (ACEs) matters so profoundly in our ministry. It's not just clinical. It's pastoral. It's spiritual.

The ACEs questionnaire is a simple but powerful tool that helps uncover the kinds of early wounds a person may carry, things like physical or emotional abuse, sexual harm, witnessing violence in the home, or living with the impact of addiction, mental illness, or the absence of a parent due to divorce or incarceration.

These experiences don't just fade away with time. When left unaddressed, they often show up years later as depression, anxiety, health problems, and broken relationships. For many in our African American communities, these silent wounds increase vulnerability to IPV and, at the same time, create deep barriers to speaking out or seeking help. And we must go even deeper: trauma isn't always isolated to a single person. It lives in bloodlines. It's woven into our histories. Our people often carry trauma that's generational and passed down through systemic injustices like racism, poverty, and violence. These aren't just social issues. They're spiritual burdens, too.

According to the CDC:[41]

- Over half of adults have experienced at least one adverse childhood experience.
- Women and people of color are more likely to carry four or more, putting them at greater risk for long-term emotional, physical, and spiritual harm.

These are the people sitting in our pews. These are our families. These are our fellow leaders. And so, we must become listeners who are led by the Spirit—full of compassion, discernment, and courage. Behind every behavior is a story. And behind every story is a soul deeply loved by God.

Discussion Questions

1. *Where have you seen signs of unhealed childhood trauma in the lives of those you shepherd, and how might the Holy Spirit be inviting you to respond differently, with sincere compassion or care?*

---

41. Centers for Disease Control and Prevention, "Adverse Childhood Experiences."

2. *How have your upbringing, family experiences, or spiritual journey shaped how you care for others, and how might healing your own story help you hold space for those in need?*

_____

_____

_____

3. *How can your church or ministry create rhythms, spaces, or practices that affirm safety, healing, and restoration for those carrying hidden or generational trauma, especially African American women impacted by IPV?*

_____

_____

_____

What Are Mandated Reporters?

As ministry leaders and caregivers, we must understand the sacred and legal responsibility that comes with being a mandated reporter. As clergy and ministry leaders, we bear both spiritual and legal responsibility. When we become aware of or suspect that a child, elder, or someone experiencing intimate partner or domestic violence is being harmed, the law requires us to report it. This isn't just a legal obligation. It's a call to protect those who are most vulnerable among us.

Professionals such as doctors, counselors, teachers, social workers, and clergy are typically included in this category, though this list is not exhaustive. For us in ministry, it's also important to be aware of the clergy-penitent privilege, which may exempt clergy from reporting when abuse is disclosed during a private or confessional conversation. However, this exemption is not recognized everywhere. States like New Hampshire, North Carolina, Oklahoma, Rhode Island, Texas, and West Virginia do not uphold this privilege in cases of child abuse.[42]

As Pentecostal clergy, we must prayerfully and wisely discern our pastoral role in these situations, honoring confidentiality where appropriate but never at the expense of protecting the vulnerable. While knowing the laws in your state is a legal duty, it is also part of your spiritual responsibility to stand with the oppressed and ensure their safety.

42. Povich, "Is the Clergy Required to Report Child Sex Abuse? Not in Some States."

RESIST RETRAUMATIZATION

Case Scenario: A Cry Behind Praise

During a midweek service, Pastor Angela notices that Sister Tamara, a faithful choir member, has been unusually quiet. Her worship is subdued, and she avoids eye contact. After service, Tamara approaches Pastor Angela and asks to speak privately. In a hushed tone, she says, "Please pray for me. Things at home have gotten tough. My husband, he gets angry. Sometimes, he throws things. Sometimes . . . he hits me. But I don't want to ruin his ministry or embarrass our family. I need prayer."

Pastor Angela feels the weight of Tamara's disclosure. She knows Tamara is not only a church member but also a mother of three and a respected figure in the congregation. She's torn between respecting Tamara's confidentiality and her role as a mandated reporter. She's also uncertain whether this disclosure falls under the clergy-penitent privilege and how that applies in her state.

Discussion Questions

1. What steps should Pastor Angela take next to ensure Tamara's safety while also honoring her legal and spiritual responsibilities?

2. How can clergy create a church culture where survivors of IPV feel safe to come forward without shame or fear of judgment?

3. How do you balance pastoral care, confidentiality, and mandatory reporting when a disclosure involves someone in leadership or ministry?

4. What local partnerships (e.g., trauma counselors, shelters, legal aid) should churches build to be ready for moments like this?

_____
_____
_____

Creating Safe, Healing Church Environments

As shepherds of God's people, we are entrusted not only with preaching the Word but also with building ministry spaces that reflect the heart of Christ: compassionate, just, and safe. When victim-survivors of trauma and IPV walk through our church doors, our systems, structures, and pastoral care should never deepen that wound. Instead, they should echo the healing presence of the Holy Spirit.

This activity invites you to begin shaping a practical expression of that healing: a trauma-informed policy. Whether it's how we welcome children, offer counsel, or invite testimony, our ministry practices must say clearly, *"Here, you are safe."*

Instructions

Begin writing a brief, trauma-informed policy draft focusing on three core areas using the prompts below.

Children's Ministry

- Who is allowed to serve in this area?
- What safety practices (e.g., background checks, check-in/out procedures) are in place to protect children?
- How will you communicate these policies to parents?

_____
_____
_____

Pastoral Counseling

- What boundaries will you set around confidentiality?
- How will you support safety planning for those disclosing IPV or trauma?
- What are your referral processes to trusted, licensed professionals?

_____
_____
_____

Public Testimonies

- How will you ensure consent and emotional readiness before someone shares their story publicly?
- What guidelines will you offer to protect both the individual and the congregation from retraumatization?

_____
_____
_____

Preaching with Care: Applying the 4Rs of Trauma-Informed Ministry to the Sermon

As Pentecostal pastors and ministers, we understand the power of the preached Word. It can break yokes, stir faith, and offer healing. But we also carry the sacred responsibility of making sure our words do not harm those who come to us wounded by trauma. Our preaching must be both Spirit-led and trauma-aware.

In this reflection, you are invited to examine a sermon of your choice: one that you've preached, heard recently, or found impactful. Through the lens of the 4Rs of trauma-informed care, Realize, Recognize, Respond, and Resist Retraumatization, you will consider how the message engages those who are carrying invisible pain, particularly survivors of intimate partner IPV and other forms of trauma.

Activity 1: Sermon Reflection—Applying the 4Rs of Trauma-Informed Care

Title: *Discerning the Heart of a Trauma-Informed Sermon*

Instructions:

1. Select a sermon of your choice. It can be one you've preached, heard from a trusted pastor, or one that's been meaningful to you in your journey. If you're unsure where to begin, consider exploring sermons by Bishop T.D. Jakes, a renowned pastor known for his powerful messages on healing, restoration, and overcoming hardship, on YouTube.

Sermon Title: _____

Preacher (if not you): _____

Date Preached/Heard: _____

2. Reflect on the sermon through the 4Rs framework:

   - **Realize:** Does the sermon show an understanding of how trauma affects individuals spiritually, emotionally, and physically?

   _____
   _____
   _____

   - **Recognize:** Are there signs of trauma acknowledged in the lives of biblical characters or people in the pews today?

   _____
   _____
   _____

   - **Respond:** How does the message offer hope, compassion, or practical encouragement to those who may be hurting?

   _____
   _____
   _____

   - **Resist Retraumatization:** Does the sermon avoid language or examples that could retraumatize survivors? Does it offer safety and dignity?

   _____
   _____
   _____

3. After completing your assessment, take a moment to pray and journal:
   - What is the Holy Spirit showing me about my preaching?
   - How can I better minister to the hearts of those silently carrying trauma?
   - What needs to shift in the way I steward the Word?

Notes: _____

_____

_____

_____

_____

_____

_____

_____

_____

_____

_____

_____

_____

_____

_____

_____

_____

Activity 2: Preaching Hope and Healing—Sharing Trauma-Informed Sermons

In this next activity, each participant will offer a brief sermon or teaching of no more than 10 minutes that thoughtfully weaves in the 4Rs of trauma-informed care: Realize, Recognize, Respond, and Resist Retraumatization. These messages should speak directly to the reality of IPV within a ministry setting, offering both pastoral care and theological insight.

Fellow clergy will listen and provide gentle, constructive feedback using an evaluation handout designed to support growth and reflection. The goal is not perfection but practice learning to preach in ways that hold both power and tenderness, truth and safety.

The facilitator or ministry leader will compile all sermons into a shared booklet, serving as a preaching toolbox to provide an ongoing resource for raising awareness and offering trauma-informed hope to our congregations.

Trauma-Informed Preaching Evaluation Form

As you listen to your colleague's sermon or teaching, use this guide to offer thoughtful feedback grounded in compassion, clarity, and the principles of trauma-informed care.

Presenter's Name: _____

Evaluator's Name: _____

Date: _____

Realize

Did the sermon demonstrate an understanding that trauma and IPV are present in the lives of many, including members of the congregation?

☐ Yes ☐ Somewhat ☐ Not clearly

Examples or Comments:

_____
_____
_____

Recognize

Did the sermon reflect an awareness of signs of trauma, language that may be triggering, or common emotional/spiritual effects of IPV?

☐ Yes ☐ Somewhat ☐ Not clearly

Examples or Comments:

_____
_____
_____

Respond

Did the message offer a compassionate, Spirit-led response that reflects the heart of Christ for those who are hurting? Were any resources, next steps, or scriptural truths offered that promote healing and safety?

☐ Yes ☐ Somewhat ☐ Not clearly

Examples or Comments:

_____
_____
_____

Resist Retraumatization

Was care taken to avoid harsh language, shaming theology, or imagery that could be harmful to survivors? Did the preacher create a spiritually safe atmosphere?

☐ Yes ☐ Somewhat ☐ Not clearly

Examples or Comments:

_____
_____
_____

Overall Strengths

What aspects of this sermon stood out as especially impactful, Spirit-led, or pastorally wise?

_____
_____
_____

Suggestions for Growth

What gentle encouragement or constructive ideas could help deepen the impact of this message in a trauma-informed way?

_____
_____
_____

Final Reflections

How did this sermon impact you personally or pastorally?

_____
_____

Transformational Conversations

As pastors and ministry leaders, we know that the work of shepherding souls is sacred and often tender. Many of the people sitting in our pews, lifting their hands in worship, or quietly lingering at the altar are carrying wounds we cannot see. Some have survived unspeakable trauma, including IPV, childhood abuse, and generational pain.

We are called to preach deliverance and healing but also to create spaces where people feel safe enough to begin the journey of restoration. That means being intentional about how we lead, listen, and care for others.

Below are some recommended tools and training to help us deepen our understanding and strengthen our ministries as trauma-informed, Spirit-led communities of healing.

Recommended Resources for Ministry Leaders

Trauma-Informed Care Training

A practical guide to help pastors and ministry teams understand how trauma affects the body, mind, and spirit and how the church can walk gently with survivors using the 4Rs: Realize, Recognize, Respond, and Resist Retraumatization.

Mental Health First Aid

This course equips leaders to recognize signs of mental health distress and respond in ways that are helpful, not harmful. It's beneficial in ministries where people are dealing with depression, anxiety, or PTSD related to past trauma.

An African American Psychology Course

This training explores how racial trauma, systemic injustice, and cultural resilience shape the mental health of Black communities. It provides faith leaders with insight and tools to care for the unique emotional and spiritual needs of African American congregations.

Resilience Leadership Course

Learn how to care for others while maintaining your emotional well-being. This course teaches strategies to help you and your church walk through grief, loss, and long-term healing together.

Best Practices for a Trauma-Informed Pentecostal Church

- Be mindful of how we use Scripture, prayer, and altar ministry, asking, "Does this heal or harm?"
- Preach with the fire of the Holy Spirit and the balm of compassion.
- Speak to the whole person's body, mind, and spirit when ministering.
- Partner with counselors, social workers, and local shelters for referrals.
- Equip lay leaders and auxiliaries to respond with empathy and wisdom.
- Offer quiet, judgment-free spaces for people to process their pain.

These training courses are often affordable and self-paced, allowing you to grow at your rhythm. More importantly, they are invitations to deepen your call to shepherd with knowledge and care.

Our goal is not just to build strong churches but to build safe ones where healing can occur, and the power of God can flow freely without

Trauma-Informed Theology

causing further harm. The Holy Spirit is not only a Comforter; he's also a Counselor. May we follow his lead with gentleness, truth, and love.

Notes: _____
_____
_____

Exit Ticket

Three things you found important.
_____
_____
_____

Two things that change your thinking.
_____
_____
_____

One thing you want to learn more about.
_____
_____
_____

Action Step

As shepherds of God's people, we are entrusted with not only preaching truth but offering refuge. Every October, communities around the country observe Domestic Violence Awareness Month, a sacred opportunity for the church to break silence, raise awareness, and offer the hope of healing to those who suffer in silence.

In our congregations, there are women, men, and children who carry the weight of intimate partner violence. Some have never spoken about it. Others are still in the middle of it. And some are walking through the slow, holy work of recovery. As Pentecostal leaders, we believe in the power of the Word to break chains and bring restoration. Still, we must also be mindful of how we preach, teach, and minister so that our pulpits become places of refuge, not retraumatization.

Activity

During October, each participant will deliver a trauma-informed sermon or Bible teaching to their congregation, small group, or auxiliary ministry. This message should reflect the 4Rs of trauma-informed ministry: realizing the impact of trauma, recognizing the signs, responding with compassion, and resisting further harm.

This is not just an assignment. It is a sacred moment to bring voice to the voiceless, light to dark places, and healing where silence has caused pain. Whether from the pulpit, in a Bible study, or during a ministry gathering, this message will help cultivate safe and Spirit-led spaces in our churches.

Let this be an offering that says to every survivor: *You are seen, you are loved, and you are not alone.*

Personal Journal of Reflection and Prayer

This journal space is an invitation to pause, reflect, and connect with yourself, with God, and with the truths that have emerged during this training. As you write, allow your thoughts, emotions, and prayers to flow freely. There is no right or wrong way to reflect; this is your sacred space for honest dialogue with your soul and your Creator.

You may consider journaling about the following:

- What stirred your Spirit during today's session?
- How is God speaking to you about your role in healing and advocacy?
- What past experiences of harm, silence, hope, or strength are surfacing?
- What prayers do you need to pray for yourself, for survivors, or for your community?

Take this time to be gentle with yourself. Let your pen become a voice of release, discovery, and prayerful commitment. Remember, healing is a journey, and reflection is a decisive step forward.

Closing Word

As we bring this work to a close, we recognize that it is more than just the end of training; this is the culmination of a comprehensive effort. It is the beginning of a clarion call for healing, justice, and transformation. The conversations we have held, the truths we've named, and the stories we've honored have opened the door to a more faithful, Spirit-led response to trauma and IPV in our communities. This journey has been about more than awareness; it's about transformation starting first in us as clergy and leaders. We have undergone a profound transformation, and what God has stirred in us here is meant to shape the way we preach, the way we shepherd, and the way we create sanctuary for those who suffer in silence.

As Pentecostal clergy, we believe in the gifts of the Spirit, the power of deliverance, and the anointing that breaks yokes. Still, we are also being called to understand how trauma binds, how it silences, and how it hides in the very places people come to be set free.

In this work, we are not just preaching sermons. We are building sanctuaries of safety. We are listening with new ears. We are resisting the cycles that wound, retraumatize, or overlook the hurting. We are responding not only with power but with mercy, discernment, and wisdom. That, too, is the work of the Holy Ghost.

The Scripture that anchors us is also the one that sends us:

> "The Spirit of the Lord is upon me, because he hath anointed me to preach the gospel to the poor; he hath sent me to heal the brokenhearted, to preach deliverance to the captives, and recovering of sight to the blind, to set at liberty them that are bruised." – Luke 4:18

Go forth in that anointing not only to speak healing but to embody it. Not only to lay hands but to hold space. And not only to prophesy but to protect.

May your ministry be both fire and balm. May your altar be both refuge and restoration. May the Holy Spirit continue to guide you as a shepherd, a healer, and a witness to the God who sees, saves, and sets free.

In his grace,
Dr. Bridget P. Robinson

About the Author

Dr. Bridget P. Robinson, a unique figure in the field of trauma-informed theology, is not just a scholar and Christian educator but also a survivor of intimate partner violence (IPV). Her journey, marked by pain, unwavering faith, and the strength never to falter, has shaped her voice and calling. This sacred journey, navigating abuse within the context of Pentecostal ministry, became the foundation for developing a trauma-informed IPV intervention tool explicitly created for Pentecostal clergy.

Born and raised in the Pentecostal tradition, Dr. Robinson continues to walk faithfully in the reformation that nurtured her. She is a licensed evangelist under Mount Calvary Holy Church of America, Inc. She has been an active member of Greater Mount Calvary Holy Church in Washington, DC, for over 25 years, serving in ministry on the Ministerial Alliance and holding leadership positions in various church ministries and initiatives. Through these experiences, she has developed a passion for pastoral care, particularly for women and children navigating the intersection of trauma and spiritual formation.

A lifelong teacher, Dr. Robinson spent more than a decade in Christian education, educating middle school students and serving as an adult educator. Her approach to ministry blends theological depth with practical compassion. As an intercessor, preacher, and advocate, she is called to teach, serve, and walk with those who have been wounded by life and overlooked by systems.

Originally from Columbia, South Carolina, Dr. Robinson relocated to Washington, DC, in the early 1990s, a move that became a turning point in her life. After escaping an abusive marriage, the city became a place of refuge and restoration. It was there that God began to rebuild her life, preparing her for ministry rooted in healing, truth, and justice. Her testimony reflects God's ability to redeem pain and transform it into purpose.

About the Author

Dr. Robinson's academic pursuits have greatly influenced her ministry and theological work. She holds a Doctor of Ministry in Spirit-filled Global Leadership in the African Diaspora from George Fox University, a Master of Arts in Health Promotion and Education from Trinity Washington University, and a Bachelor of Arts in Psychology from the University of the District of Columbia. These academic achievements have taken her to São Paulo, Brazil, and Cape Town, South Africa, shaping her understanding of global ministry and cultural competency. She is also the author of *My Eyes Dare to Believe* and *A Single Woman's Guide to Protecting and Defending Her Celibacy in God*.

Today, Dr. Robinson continues to teach and serve with authenticity and love. She is the proud mother of two adult children and a grandmother. Her mission is clear: to break generational cycles of abuse, equip leaders to respond with compassion, and transform the Church into a true sanctuary, a place where healing, safety, and Spirit-filled transformation are not just preached but practiced.

Bibliography

Abernethy, Alexis D. "Women's Leadership in the African American Church." Fuller Studio, June 6, 2015. https://fullerstudio.fuller.edu/womens-leadership-in-the-african-american-church.

Alexander, Estrelda Y. *Black Fire: One Hundred Years of African American Pentecostalism.* Downers Grove, IL: InterVarsity, 2011.

Al'uqdah, Shareefah N., et al. "Intimate Partner Violence in the African American Community: Risk, Theory, and Interventions." *Journal of Family Violence* 31, no. 7 (2016) 877–84. ProQuest.

Anda, Robert F., et al. "The Enduring Effects of Abuse and Related Adverse Experiences in Childhood: A Convergence of Evidence from Neurobiology and Epidemiology." *European Archives of Psychiatry and Clinical Neuroscience* 256, no. 3 (2006) 174–186. https://www.proquest.com/scholarly-journals/enduring-effects-abuse-related-adverse/docview/214161873/se-2.

Anyabwile, Thabiti. "This Black Pastor Led a White Church—in 1788." Christianity Today, May 23, 2017. https://www.christianitytoday.com/history/2017/may/lemuel-haynes-pioneering-african-american-pastor.html.

Astley, Jeff. *Ordinary Theology: Looking, Listening and Learning in Theology.* New York: Routledge, 2002.

Bailey, Anne C. *African Voices of the Atlantic Slave Trade: Beyond the Silence and the Shame.* Boston: Beacon, 2006.

Baldwin, Jennifer. "Trauma-Sensitive Theology, Jennifer Baldwin Interview." Wipf and Stock, January 15, 2019, YouTube video, 14:55. https://youtu.be/z8RAGfBz9gk.

———. *Trauma-Sensitive Theology: Thinking Theologically in the Era of Trauma.* Eugene, OR: Cascade, 2018.

Barfoot, Charles H., and Gerald T. Sheppard. "Prophetic vs. Priestly Religion: The Changing Role of Women Clergy in Classical Pentecostal Churches." *Review of Religious Research* 22, no. 1 (1980) Exlibris.

Barrick, Audrey. "Survey: 1 in 4 U.S. Christians Identify as Pentecostal." *The Christian Post*, March 29, 2010. https://www.christianpost.com/news/survey-young-christians-embrace-spiritual-gifts-lack-theological-depth.html.

Bell, Carl C., and Jacqueline Mattis. "The Importance of Cultural Competence in Ministering to African American Victims of Domestic Violence." *Violence Against Women* 6, no. 5 (May 2000) 515–32, ProQuest.

Bent-Goodley Tricia, et al., "Perceptions, Help-Seeking, and High-Risk Domestic Violence in Black Communities." *Journal of Interpersonal Violence* 38, no. 15–16 (2023) 9536–62. doi: 10.1177/08862605231168814.

BIBLIOGRAPHY

Best Skills. "Trauma Informed Care for Leadership Crash Course." Udemy Online Course, October 2022. https://www.udemy.com/user/best-skills.

Bethlehem Apostolic Church. "Pentecostal Assemblies of the World, Inc. Elect First Female Member to Executive Bishops' Council." *Cision PR Newswire.* Accessed December 11, 2022. https://www.prnewswire.com/news-releases/pentecostal-assemblies-of-the-world-inc-elect-first-female-member-to-executive-bishops-council-301606937.html.

Bidwell, Duane R. "Developing an Adequate 'Pneumatraumatology': Understanding the Spiritual Impacts of Traumatic Injury." *The Journal of Pastoral Care & Counseling* 56, no. 2 (2002) 135–43. Exlibris.

Bingemer, Maria Clara. "Reflection on the Trinity." In *Through Her Eyes: Women's Theology from Latin America,* edited by Elsa Tamez, 57–69. Maryknoll, NY: Orbis Books, 1989.

Blessett, Brandi and Vanessa Littleton. "Examining the Impact of Institutional Racism in Black Residentially Segregated Communities." *Ralph Bunche Journal of Public Affairs* 6, No. 1, (2017) http://digitalscholarship.tsu.edu/rbjpa/vol6/iss1/3.

Blevins, Sonya. "Learning Styles: The Impact on Education." *Medsurg Nursing* 30, no. 4 (2021) 285–86.

Bloom, Benjamin S., ed. *Taxonomy of Educational Objectives: The Classification of Educational Goals.* Handbook I: Cognitive Domain. New York: David McKay, 1956.

Boserup, Brad, et al. "Alarming Trends in U.S. Domestic Violence During the COVID-19 Pandemic." *The American Journal of Emergency Medicine* 38, no. 12 (December 2020) 2753–55. https://doi.org/10.1016/j.ajem.2020.04.077.

Bourna, Jeremy. "Is the Bible 'Patriarchal'? Yes and No—An Excerpt from Gender Roles and the People of God." *Zondervan Academic* (blog), August 29, 2017. https://zondervanacademic.com/blog/is-the-bible-patriarchal-yes-and-no-an-excerpt-from-gender-roles-and-the-people-of-god.

Breiding, Matthew J. "Prevalence and Characteristics of Sexual Violence, Stalking, and Intimate Partner Violence Victimization—National Intimate Partner and Sexual Violence Survey, United States, 2011." *American Journal of Public Health* 105, no. 4 (April 2015) E11–12, ProQuest.

Breiding, Matthew J., et al. "Intimate Partner Violence in the United States—2010." Centers for Disease Control and Prevention. 2014. https://stacks.cdc.gov/view/cdc/21961.

Brice-Baker, Janet R. "Domestic Violence in African American and African-Caribbean Families." *Journal of Social Distress and Homelessness* 3, no. 1 (1994): 23–38.

Burke Harris, Nadine. *The Deepest Well: Healing the Long-Term Effects of Childhood Adversity.* Boston: Mariner, 2019.

Burke, Nadine. J., et al. "The Impact of Adverse Childhood Experiences on an Urban Pediatric Population." *Child Abuse & Neglect,* 35, no. 6, (June 2011) 408–13. https://doi.org/10.1016/j.chiabu.2011.02.006.

Burt, Wava. "Tamar: Girl Next Door II Samuel 13: 1–22." *Journal of Religion & Abuse* 3, no. 3–4 (2002) 143–49. Exlibris.

Butler-King, Renea. "Identifying Intergenerational Transmission of Historical Trauma Using the Genogram Psychosocial Assessment Tool" *SHAREOK Repository* (2021). Exlibris.

Capaldi, Deborah M., et al. "A Systematic Review of Risk Factors for Intimate Partner Violence." *Partner Abuse* 3, no. 2 (2012) 231–80. https://doi.org/10.1891/1946-6560.3.2.231.

Bibliography

Carr, David M. *Holy Resilience: The Bible's Traumatic Origins.* New Haven, CT: Yale University Press, 2014.

Carter, Selina D. "The Voice of Silence: Domestic Violence and the African American Church Response." DMin diss., New Brunswick Theological Seminary, 2020. https://www.proquest.com/docview/2404036017.

Centers of Disease Control and Prevention, "Adverse Childhood Experiences," Vital Signs, August 23, 2021, https://www.cdc.gov/vitalsigns/aces/index.html.

———. *"Data Collection Methods for Program Evaluation: Focus Groups."* Centers for Disease Control and Prevention. 2008. https://www.cdc.gov/healthyyouth/evaluation/pdf/brief13.pdf.

———. "Fast Facts: Preventing Intimate Partner Violence." Centers for Disease Control and Prevention. Accessed April 22, 2022. https://www.cdc.gov/violenceprevention/intimatepartnerviolence/fastfact.html.

———. "Risk Protective Factors for Perpetration." Centers for Disease Control and Prevention. Accessed January 16, 2023. https://www.cdc.gov/violenceprevention/intimatepartnerviolence/riskprotectivefactors.html.

———. "Take A Stand Against Domestic Violence." Injury Prevention and Control. October 20, 2021. https://www.cdc.gov/injury/features/intimate-partner-violence/index.html.

Coates, Ta-Nehisi. "The Case for Reparations." *The Atlantic*, June 2014. https://www.theatlantic.com/magazine/archive/2014/06/the-case-for-reparations/361631/.

Cross, Terry L., et al. "A Monograph on Effective Services for Minority Children Who Are Severely Emotionally Disturbed." *Towards a Culturally Competent System of Care*, 1. (1989) 1–90. https://files.eric.ed.gov/fulltext/ED330171.pdf.

Daniels, David III. "1619 and The Arrival of African Christianity," *McCormick Theological Seminary*, September 3, 2019. https://www.mccormick.edu/news/1619-and-the-arrival-of-african-christianity.

Danticat, Edwidge. "We Are Ugly, But We Are Here." *The Caribbean Writer* 10 (1996). http://faculty.webster.edu/corbetre/haiti/literature/danticat-ugly.htm.

Danzer, Graham. "African Americans' Historical Trauma: Manifestations in and Outside of Therapy." *Journal of Theory Construction & Testing* 16, no. 1 (July 2012) 16–21. ProQuest.

Davis, Maxine, et al. "Exploring Black Clergy Perspectives on Religious/Spiritual Related Domestic Violence: First Steps in Facing Those Who Wield the Sword Abusively." *Journal of Aggression, Maltreatment & Trauma* 30, no. 7 (2021) 950–71. Exlibris.

Decker, Michele R., et al. "Prevalence and Health Impact of Intimate Partner Violence and Non-partner Sexual Violence Among Female Adolescents Aged 15–19 Years in Vulnerable Urban Environments: A Multi-Country Study." *Journal of Adolescent Health* 55, no. 6 (December 2014): S58–67. https://www-sciencedirect-com.georgefox.idm.oclc.org/science/article/pii/S1054139X14003541.

DeGruy, Joy. *Post-Traumatic Slave Syndrome: America's Legacy of Enduring Injury and Healing.* Rev. ed. Portland, OR: Joy DeGruy, 2017.

Domestic Abuse Intervention Programs. *Power and Control: Creating a Process of Change for Men Who Batter (Supplement to the Duluth Curriculum).* Duluth, MN: Domestic Abuse Intervention Programs, January 2023. https://www.theduluthmodel.org/wp-content/uploads/2023/01/CMCL-PC.pdf

Domestic Abuse Intervention Programs. "Power and Control Wheel." Duluth, MN: Domestic Abuse Intervention Programs, March 2017. https://www.theduluthmodel.org/wp-content/uploads/2017/03/PowerandControl.pdf.

Drescher, Seymour. "The Atlantic Slave Trade and the Holocaust: A Comparative Analysis." In Is the Holocaust Unique? *Routledge* 3rd ed., (2009) 103–23. Exlibris.

Drumm, Rene D., et al. "Clergy Training for Effective Response to Intimate Partner Violence Disclosure: Immediate and Long-Term Benefits." *Journal of Religion & Spirituality in Social Work* 37, no. 1 (2018) 77–93.

Dumitrascu, Sorin. "ADDIE: A Guide for Training and Development Professionals." Udemy, August 2023. https://www.udemy.com/user/sorindumitrascu/.

Elearning Infographics. "The Adult Learning Theory—Andragogy—Infographic." Elearning Infographics. Accessed October 28, 2023. https://elearninginfographics.com/adult-learning-theory-andragogy-infographic/.

———. "Knowles' 5 Assumptions of Adult Learners." Elearning Infographics. Accessed October 28, 2023. https://elearninginfographics.com/adult-learning-theory-andragogy-infographic/.

Encyclopedia Britannica. "Patriarchy." Encyclopedia Britannica. Accessed November 22, 2023. https://www.britannica.com/topic/patriarchy.

Errendal, Sofie. "Figure The Hermeneutic Loop." Research Gate. Accessed December 15, 2023. https://www.researchgate.net/figure/The-Hermeneutic-Loop_fig1_333843805.

Espinosa, Gaston. *William J. Seymour and the Origins of Global Pentecostalism: A Biography and Documentary History.* Durham: Duke University Press, 2014.

Eyerman, Ron. *Cultural Trauma: Slavery and the Formation of African American Identity.* Cambridge, MA: Cambridge University Press, 2001. eBook, Exlibris.

Felder, Pamela Petrease, "The Philosophical Approach of Sankofa: Perspectives on Historically Marginalized Doctoral Students in the United States and South Africa," *International Journal of Doctoral Studies* (2019), https://www.researchgate.net/publication/344658628.

Felitti, Vincent J., et al. "Relationship of Childhood Abuse and Household Dysfunction to Many of the Leading Causes of Death in Adults: The Adverse Childhood Experiences (ACE) Study." *American Journal of Preventive Medicine* 14, no. 4 (1998) 245–58. https://doi.org/10.1016/S0749-3797(98)00017-8.

Gabaitse, Rosianah M. "Pentecostal Hermeneutics and the Marginalization of Women." *Scriptura*, 114, no. 1 (2015) 1–12. EBSCOhost.

Gardner, Tselane. "It Takes a Village: African American Psychology." Udemy Online Course, February 2021. https://www.udemy.com/user/tselane-gardner.

Gecewicz, Claire. "Few Americans Say Their House of Worship Is Open, But a Quarter Say Their Faith Has Grown Amid Pandemic." Pew Research Center, April 30, 2020. https://www.pewresearch.org/fact-tank/2020/04/30/few-americans-say-their-house-of-worship-is-open-but-a-quarter-say-their-religious-faith-has-grown-amid-pandemic/.

Gillum, Tameka L. "African American Survivors of Intimate Partner Violence: Lived Experience and Future Directions for Research." *Journal of Aggression, Maltreatment & Trauma* 30, no. 6 (June 2021) 731–48. https://doi-org.georgefox.idm.oclc.org/10.1080/10926771.2019.1607962.

———. "The Benefits of a Culturally Specific Intimate Partner Violence Intervention for African American Survivors." *Violence Against Women* 14, no. 8 (2008) 917–43. Exlibris.

———. "Exploring the Link Between Stereotypic Images and Intimate Partner Violence in the African American Community." *Violence Against Women* 8, no. 1 (January 2002) 64–86. https://doi-org.georgefox.idm.oclc.org/10.1177/10778010222182946.

———. "The Intersection of Intimate Partner Violence and Poverty in Black Communities." *Aggression and Violent Behavior* 46 (May–June 2019) 37. https://www.proquest.com/docview/2263311006.

Goddard-Eckrich, Dawn, et al. "Evidence of Help-Seeking Behaviors Among Black Women Under Community Supervision in New York City: A Plea for Culturally Tailored Intimate Partner Violence Interventions." *Women's Health Reports* 3, no. 1 (2022) 867–76. Exlibris.

Greer, Teylar, "Racial-Trauma Informed Ministry: A Process for Dominant Culture Ministries to Effectively Engage with Communities Impacted by Racial Trauma" *Seattle Pacific Seminary Projects*, 2017. https://digitalcommons.spu.edu/spseminary_projects/4.

Groome, Thomas H. *Sharing Faith: A Comprehensive Approach to Religious Education and Pastoral Ministry: The Way of Shared Praxis*. Eugene, OR: Wipf and Stock, 1991.

Gump, Janice P. "Reality Matters: The Shadow of Trauma on African American Subjectivity." *Psychoanalytic Psychology* 27, no. 1 (2010): 42–54. Exlibris.

Haahr-Pedersen, Ida, et al. "Females Have More Complex Patterns of Childhood Adversity: Implications for Mental, Social, and Emotional Outcomes in Adulthood." *European Journal of Psychotraumatology* 11, no. 1 (2020). https://www.proquest.com/scholarly-journals/females-have-more-complex-patterns-childhood/docview/2492475335/se-2.

Hamence, Erica. "What Does Making the Church Safer Look Like?" *St. Mark's Review*, no. 243 (2018): 98–113. Exlibris.

Hampton, Robert, et al. "Domestic Violence in the African American Community: An Analysis of Social and Structural Factors." *Violence Against Women* 9, no. 5 (May 2003) 533–57. https://doi.org/10.1177/1077801202250450.

Hannah-Jones, Nikole. *The 1619 Project: A New Origin Story*. New York: One World, 2021.

Harris, Antipas L., and Michael D. Palmer. *The Holy Spirit and Social Justice, Interdisciplinary Global Perspectives: History, Race, and Culture*. Lanham, MD: Seymour, 2019.

Haughee, Chris. *Bruised Reeds and Smoldering Wicks*. New Providence, NJ: Bowker Identifier Services, 2019.

Hays-Grudo, Jennifer, and Amanda Sheffield Morris. *Adverse and Protective Childhood Experiences: A Developmental Perspective*. Washington, D.C.: American Psychological Association, 2020.

Henderson, Zuleka R., et al. "Conceptualizing Healing Through the African American Experience of Historical Trauma." *American Journal of Orthopsychiatry* 91, no. 6 (2021) 763–75. Exlibris.

Hicks, Shari Renee. "A Critical Analysis of Post Traumatic Slave Syndrome: A Multigenerational Legacy of Slavery." Psy.D, California Institute of Integral Studies, 2015. https://www.proquest.com/docview/1707689965.

Hinds, Sonia. "Spiritual Justice: Towards a Womanish Spirituality of Spiritual Care." In *The Holy Spirit and Social Justice, Interdisciplinary Global Perspectives—History,*

Race, and Culture. Edited by Antipas L. Harris and Michael D. Palmer. Lanham, MD: Seymour, 2019.

History.com. "Women's Suffrage." History.com. Accessed November 13, 2023. https://www.history.com/topics/womens-history/the-fight-for-womens-suffrage.

Houston-Kolnik, Jaclyn and Nathan R. Todd. "Examining the Presence of Congregational Programs Focused on Violence Against Women." *American Journal of Community Psychology* 57, no. 3 (June 2016) 459–72, https://www.proquest.com/docview/2057242054.

Humphreys, Colin J., and W. G. Waddington. "The Jewish Calendar, A Lunar Eclipse and the Date of Christ's Crucifixion." *Tyndale Bulletin* 43, no. 2 (1992) 331–51, ProQuest.

Hunsinger, Deborah van Deusen. "Trauma-Informed Spiritual Care: Lifelines for a Healing Journey." *Theology Today*, 77, no. 4, 359–71. https://doi-org.georgefox.idm.oclc.org/10.1177/0040573620961145.

Huxley, Ron. "The Trauma Toolkit." Thinkific. Accessed March 16, 2022. https://ronhuxley.thinkific.com/courses/traumatoolbox.

Jacobs, Michelle S. "The Violent State: Black Women's Invisible Struggle Against Police Violence." *William & Mary Journal of Race, Gender and Social Justice* 39 (2017), https://scholarship.law.wm.edu/wmjowl/vol24/iss1/4.

Jakes, Thomas D. *Don't Drop the Mic: The Power of Your Words Can Change the World.* New York: FaithWords, 2021.

———. "Surviving the Trauma of Rejection and Abandonment Plan." The Potter's House, August 4, 2022, YouTube video, 1:11:32. https://youtu.be/KgE_ugEnm3Q.

———. "Trauma, Triggers, and Triumph." The Potter's House, January 17, 2021, YouTube video, 1:21:46. https://youtu.be/HzujSUnYUyQ.

Jones, Serene. *Trauma and Grace: Theology in a Ruptured World*, 2nd ed. Louisville, KY: Westminster John Knox, 2019.

Keil and Delitzsch Old Testament Commentary. "Deuteronomy 21." Bible Hub. Accessed December 6, 2023. https://biblehub.com/commentaries/kad/deuteronomy/21.htm.

King, Fergus J., and Dorothy A. Lee. "Lost in Translation: Rethinking Words About Women in 1-2 Timothy." *Scottish Journal of Theology* 74, no. 1 (February 2021) 52–66. https://www.proquest.com/scholarly-journals/lost-translation-rethinking-words-about-women-1-2/docview/2501228774/se-2.

Kissi, Samuel Baah, et al. "The Philisophy of Adinkra Symbols in Asante Textiles, Jewellery and Other Art Forms." *Journal of Asian Scientific Research* 9, no. 4 (2019) 29–39. https://doi.org/10.18488/journal.2.2019.94.29.39.

Knowles, Malcolm S. *Andragogy in Action* 1st ed. San Francisco: Jossey-Bass, 1984.

Kolk, Bessel van der. *The Body Keeps the Score: Mind, Brain, and Body in the Transformation of Trauma.* London: Penguin Books, 2014.

Krotz, Kathryn C. "Trauma-Informed Ministry: A Framework and Recommendations for Training for Christian Ministry Workers." Doctor of Ministry Dissertation, Fuller Theological Seminary, 2019. https://www.proquest.com/dissertations-theses/trauma-informed-ministry-framework/docview/2246006055/se-2.

Kumar, Shanath. "Adult Learning and Instructional Design Model for Trainers." Online Course presented at Udemy, February 2023. https://www.udemy.com/user/shanathkumar/.

Kurt, Serhat. "Addie Model: Instructional Design." Educational Technology, August 29, 2017. https://educationaltechnology.net/the-addie-model-instructional-design/.

———. "Dick and Carey Instructional Model." Educational Technology, November 23, 2015. https://educationaltechnology.net/dick-and-carey-instructional-model/.

BIBLIOGRAPHY

Langford, Joy. "Feminism and Leadership in the Pentecostal Movement." *Feminist Theology* 26, no. 1 (2017) 69–79. Exlibris.

Lin, Luona, et al. "How Diverse Is the Psychology Workforce?" American Psychology Association, February 2018. https://www.apa.org/monitor/2018/02/datapoint.

Majors, Richard, and Janet Mancini Billson, *Cool Pose: The Dilemmas of Black Manhood in America*. New York: Lexington, 1992.

Malan, Gert J. "God's Patronage Constitutes a Community of Compassionate Equals." *Hervormde Teologiese Studies* 76, no. 4 (2020). https://doi.org/10.4102/hts.v76i4.5989.

Mamiya, L. H. "The Labor of Faith: Gender and Power in Black Apostolic Pentecostalism." *Choice* 55, no. 3 (November 2017): 359, https://www.proquest.com/trade-journals/labor-faith-gender-power-black-apostolic/docview/1953877053/se-2.

Manetta, Ameda A., et al. "The Church-Does It Provide Support for Abused Women? Differences in the Perceptions of Battered Women and Parishioners." *Journal of Religion & Abuse* 5, no. 1 (2003) 5–21. Exlibris.

Masci, David. "5 Facts about the Religious Lives of African Americans." Pew Research Center, February 7, 2018. https://www.pewresearch.org/fact-tank/2018/02/07/5-facts-about-the-religious-lives-of-african-americans/.

McDonald, Joseph. "Hermeneutics of Trauma and the Bible." Oxford Bibliographies, September 26, 2022. https://www.oxfordbibliographies.com/display/document/obo-9780195393361/obo-9780195393361-0303.xml.

Menakem, Resmaa. *My Grandmother's Hands: Racialized Trauma and the Pathway to Mending Our Hearts and Bodies*. Las Vegas: Central Recovery Press, 2017.

Merriam, Sharan B. *Qualitative Research: A Guide to Design and Implementation*. Revised and Expanded. San Francisco, CA: John Wiley & Son, 2009.

Metta Healing Oasis. "The Seven Psychological Strengths of African Americans by Dr. Joseph L. White." Metta Healing Oasis. Accessed May 27, 2023. https://www.mettahealingoasis.com/SEVEN_PSYCHOLOGICAL_STRENGTHS_OF_AFRICAN_AMERICANS1.pdf.

National Alliance on Mental Illness. "Mental Health in African American Communities: Challenges, Resources, Community Voices." National Alliance on Mental Illness. Accessed November 10, 2020. https://namica.org/mental-health-challengesinafricanamerican-communities/.

National Center For PTSD. "How Common is PTSD in Adults?" U.S. Department of Veterans Affairs. Accessed December 30, 2023, https://www.ptsd.va.gov/understand/common/common_adults.asp.

National Child Traumatic Stress Network. "Trauma-Informed Care." The National Child Traumatic Stress Network. Accessed November 28, 2021. https://www.nctsn.org/trauma-informed-care.

National Coalition Against Domestic Violence. "The Nation's Leading Grassroots Voice on Domestic Violence." National Coalition Against Domestic Violence. Accessed November 8, 2021. https://ncadv.org/.

National Council for Behavioral Health, *Mental Health First Aid USA, Participant Processing Guide, Adult*. Washington, D.C.: National Council for Behavioral Health, 2015.

BIBLIOGRAPHY

National Park Service. "Akoma Ntoso—Understanding." National Park Service. Accessed October 21, 2023. https://www.nps.gov/afbg/learn/historyculture/akoma-ntoso.htm.

———. "Denkyem—Adaptability." National Park Service. Accessed October 21, 2023. https://www.nps.gov/afbg/learn/historyculture/denkyem.htm.

———. "Gye Nyame—Supremacy of God." National Park Service. Accessed October 21, 2023. https://www.nps.gov/afbg/learn/historyculture/gye-nyame.htm.

———. "Matie Masie—Wisdom and Prudence." National Park Service. Accessed October 21, 2023. https://www.nps.gov/afbg/learn/historyculture/matie-masie.htm.

———. "Nsoromma—Guardianship." National Park Service. Accessed October 21, 2023. https://www.nps.gov/afbg/learn/historyculture/nsoromma.htm.

———. "Sankofa—Learn from the Past." National Park Service. Accessed October 21, 2023. https://www.nps.gov/afbg/learn/historyculture/sankofa.htm.

Nelms Smarr, Kimberly, et al. "Gender and Race in Ministry Leadership: Experiences of Black Clergywomen." *Religions* 9, no. 12 (2018) 377. https://doi.org/10.3390/rel9120377.

Nkomazana, Fidelis. "The Role of Women, Theology, and Ecumenical Organizations in the Rise of Pentecostal Churches in Botswana." In *Pentecostalism and Politics in Africa*, 181–202.

O'Doherty, Kevin. "Introduction to PTSD." Udemy, February 2019. https://www.udemy.com/user/kevinmichaelodoherty.

Oden, Thomas C. *How Africa Shaped the Christian Mind, Rediscovering the African Seedbed of Western Christianity.* Downers Grove, IL: InterVarsity, 2007.

Pack, Stephen Michael. "Equipping Evangelical Leaders to Address Domestic Abuse in the Local Church." Doctor of Ministry Dissertation, Southeastern Baptist Theological Seminary, 2020. https://www.proquest.com/dissertations-theses/equipping-evangelical-leaders-address-domestic/docview/2468393130/se-2.

Panchal, Nirmita, Rabah Kamal, and Cynthia Cox. "The Implications of COVID-19 for Mental Health and Substance Use." Kaiser Family Foundation, February 10, 2021. https://www.kff.org/coronavirus-covid-19/issue-brief/the-implications-of-covid-19-for-mental-health-and-substance-use/.

Payne, Beth. "Resilience Leadership." Udemy Online Course, November 2021. https://www.udemy.com/user/beth-payne-6.

Perry, Ruth. "10 Awesome Women Pastors from History." CBE International (blog), March 7, 2018. https://www.cbeinternational.org/resource/10-awesome-women-pastors-history/

Petrease Felder, Pamela. "The Philosophical Approach of Sankofa: Perspectives on Historically Marginalized Doctoral Students in the United States and South Africa." *International Journal of Doctoral Studies* (2019). https://www.researchgate.net/publication/344658628.

Petrosky, Emiko, et al. "Racial and Ethnic Differences in Homicides of Adult Women and the Role of Intimate Partner Violence—United States, 2003–2014." *MMWR. Morbidity and Mortality Weekly Report; Atlanta* 66, no. 28 (July 2017), https://www.proquest.com/reports/racial-ethnic-differences-homicides-adult-women/docview/1923968551/se-2.

Pew Research Center. "The New Face of Global Christianity: The Emergence of Progressive Pentecostalism." Pew Research Center, April 12, 2006. https://www.pewresearch.

org/religion/2006/04/12/the-new-face-of-global-christianity-the-emergence-of-progressive-pentecostalism.

Phillips, Anita. "A Spiritual Approach to Trauma Recovery." Essence Wellness House Event, April 17, 2020, YouTube video, 32:16. https://youtu.be/h2RH0RW2Tcg.

Ponton, David, I., II. "Private Matters in Public Spaces: Intimate Partner Violence Against Black Women in Jim Crow Houston." *Frontiers* 39, no. 2 (2018) 58–96, https://www.proquest.com/docview/2059593965.

Povich, Elaine S. "Is the Clergy Required to Report Child Sex Abuse? Not in Some States." Governing, January 24, 2019. https://www.governing.com/archive/sl-clergy-sex-abuse-reporting-states.html.

Powell, John A. "The Impact of Societal Systems on Black Male Violence." *Journal of Aggression, Maltreatment & Trauma* 16, no. 3 (2008) 311–29, https://www.proquest.com//docview/61667363.

Pruitt, Sarah. "What Part of Africa Did Most Enslaved People Come From?" History.com. Accessed December 11, 2023. https://www.history.com/news/what-part-of-africa-did-most-slaves-come-from.

Pyles, Loretta. "The Complexities of the Religious Response to Domestic Violence: Implications for Faith-Based Initiatives." *Affilia* 22, no. 3 (2007) 281–91. Exlibris.

Rambo, Shelly. *Resurrecting Wounds: Living in the Afterlife of Trauma*. Waco, TX: Baylor University Press, 2018.

———. *Spirit and Trauma: A Theology of Remaining*. Louisville, KY: Westminster John Knox, 2010.

Recovery Village, The. "Important Facts and Statistics About PTSD (Post-Traumatic Stress Disorder)." *The Recovery Village*, August 30, 2024. https://www.therecoveryvillage.com/mental-health/ptsd/ptsd-statistics/

Richard, Carlos Jermaine, "Intimate Partner Violence in the Black Church: Bridging the Gap between Awareness and Policy Development" DMin diss., George Fox University, 2015. https://digitalcommons.georgefox.edu/dmin/110.

Richardson, Elaine. "'She Was Workin like Foreal': Critical Literacy and Discourse Practices of African American Females in the Age of Hip Hop." *Discourse & Society* 18, no. 6 (November 2007) 789–809. https://doiorg.georgefox.idm.oclc.org/10.1177/0957926507082197.

Robeck, Cecil M. "Women in Pentecostal Movement." Fuller Studio. Accessed December 10, 2022. https://fullerstudio.fuller.edu/women-in-the-pentecostal-movement/.

Salisbury, J. Ellen. "Perpetua." *Encyclopedia Britannica*. Accessed March 3, 2023. https://www.britannica.com/biography/Perpetua-Christian-martyr.

Sanchez Walsh, Arlene M. *Pentecostals in America*. New York: Columbia University, 2018.

Sancken, Joni, S. *All Our Griefs to Bear: Responding with Resilience after Collective Trauma*. Harrisonburg, VA: Herald, 2022.

Sande, Nomatter. "Faith and Equality: Rethinking Women in Leadership Positions in Pentecostalism." *Journal of Gender and Religion in Africa* 22, no.1 (July 2017) 50–62. https://www.researchgate.net/publication/326247531_Faith_and_Equality_Rethinking_Women_in_Leadership_Positions_in_Pentecostalism.

———. "The Pentecostal Theology and Gender-based Violence." *International Journal of Contemporary Applied Researches* 6, no. 2 (2019) 1–12. https://www.researchgate.net/profile/Nomatter-Sande/publication/332246703_The_Pentecostal_Theology_and_Gender-Based_Violence.

Saul, Steven. *The Response of the Church to Domestic Violence: A Silent or Active Voice to Broken Families*. PDF file. June 2011. https://rts.edu/wpcontent/uploads/2019/05/201106-Saul-Steven.pdf.

Schmidt, Kelly L. "Strategic Leadership as Modeled by the Daughters of Zelophehad." *Journal of Biblical Perspectives in Leadership* 10, no. 1 (2020) 102–12.

Schussler Fiorenza, Elisabeth. *But She Said: Feminist Practices of Biblical Interpretation*. Boston: Beacon, 1992.

Scott-Jones, Gwendolyn, and Mozella Richardson Kamara. "The Traumatic Impact of Structural Racism on African Americans." *Delaware Journal of Public Health* 6, no. 5 (2020) 80–82. Exlibris.

Seleina Parsitau, Damaris. "Soft Tongue, Powerful Voice, Huge Influence: The Dynamics of Gender, Soft Power, and Political Influence in Faith Evangelistic Ministries in Kenya." In *Pentecostalism and Politics in Africa*, 159–80. London: Palgrave Macmillan, 2018.

Shabatura, Jessica. "Using Bloom's Taxonomy to Write Effective Learning Outcomes." University of Arkansas, July 26, 2022. https://tips.uark.edu/using-blooms-taxonomy/.

Smarr, Kimberly Nelms, Rachelle Disbennett-Lee, and Amy Cooper Hakim, "Gender and Race in Ministry Leadership: Experiences of Black Clergywomen," *Religions* 9, no. 12 (2018): 377. https://doi.org/10.3390/rel9120377.

Smith, S.G., et al. "The National Intimate Partner and Sexual Violence Survey: 2010–2012 State Report." National Center for Injury Prevention and Control, 2017, 117–118. https://www.cdc.gov/violenceprevention/pdf/NISVS-StateReportBook.pdf.

Soares, Judith. "Eden after Eve: Christian Fundamentalism and Women in Barbados." In *Nation Dance: Religion, Identity, and Cultural Difference in the Caribbean*, edited by Patrick Taylor. Bloomington: Indiana University Press, 2001, EBSCOhost.

Spencer, Aída Besançon. *Beyond the Curse: Women Called to Ministry*. Nashville: Thomas Nelson Publishers, 1985.

Stennis, Kesslyn Brade, et al. "The Development of a Culturally Competent Intimate Partner Violence Intervention- S.T.A.R.T.©: Implications for Competency-Based Social Work Practice." *Social Work and Christianity* 42, no. 1 (Spring 2015) 96–109. https://www.proquest.com/scholarly-journals/development-culturally-competent-intimate-partner/docview/1655810551/se-2.

Stockman, J.K., et al. "Intimate Partner Violence and its Health Impact on Ethnic Minority Women." *Journal of Women's Health*, 24, no. 1 (December 2014) 62–79. https://doi.org/10.1089/jwh.2014.4879.

Stückelberger, Christoph, and Jesse Mugambi, eds. "Responsible Leadership: Global and Contextual Ethical Perspectives." Globethics.net, 2007, 3–12. https://www.globethics.net/documents/10131/26882154/GlobalSerie_1_ResponsibleLeadership_text.pdf/.

Substance Abuse and Mental Health Services Administration. *SAMHSA's Concept of Trauma and Guidance for a Trauma-Informed Approach*. HHS Publication No. (SMA) 14-4884. Rockville, MD: Substance Abuse and Mental Health Services Administration, 2014.

Taft, Casey T., et al. "Intimate Partner Violence Against African American Women: An Examination of the Socio-Cultural Context." *Aggression and Violent Behavior: A Review Journal* 14, no. 1 (2009) 50–58, ProQuest.

Thomas, John. "Women, Pentecostals, and the Bible: An Experiment in Pentecostal Hermeneutics." *Journal of Pentecostal Theology* 2, no. 5 (1994) 41–56. Exlibris.

Bibliography

Thompson, Curt. *Anatomy of the Soul: Surprising Connection Between Neuroscience and Spiritual Practices That Can Transform Your Life and Relationship*. Carol Stream, IL: Tyndale Refresh, 2010.

Thompson, M. P., et al. "Partner Violence, Social Support, and Distress among Inner-City African American Women." *American Journal of Community Psychology* 28, no. 1 (February 2000) 127–43, https://www.proquest.com/docview/57825821.

Thurmond-Malone, Myrna Latrice. *Midwifing—A Womanist Approach to Pastoral Counseling: Investigating the Fractured Self, Slavery, Violence, and the Black Woman*. Eugene, OR: Pickwick, 2019.

TraumaInformed.com. "Trauma-Informed Churches." TraumaInformed.com. Accessed April 5, 2022. https://www.traumainformedmd.com/churches.html.

Travis, Sarah. *Unspeakable: Preaching and Trauma-Informed Theology*. Eugene, OR: Cascade, 2021.

United Nations. "Declaration on the Elimination of Violence against Women Proclaimed by General Assembly Resolution 48/104 of December 20, 1993." United Nations. https://www.un.org/en/genocideprevention/documents/atrocitycrimes/Doc.21_declaration%20elimination%20vaw.pdf.

———. "Home, the Most Dangerous Place for Women, with Majority of Female Homicide Victims Worldwide Killed by Partners or Family, UNODC Study Says." United Nations. Accessed April 12, 2022. https://www.unodc.org/unodc/en/press/releases/2018/November/home--the-most-dangerous-place-for-women--with-majority-of-female-homicide-victims-worldwide-killed-by-partners-or-family--unodc-study-says.html.

Valamis. "Learning Theories, Adult Learning Principles." Valamis. Accessed October 28, 2023. https://www.valamis.com/hub/adult-learning-principles.

Vernor, Dale. "PTSD is More Likely in Women Than Men." National Alliance of Mental Illness, October 8, 2019. https://www.nami.org/Blogs/NAMI-Blog/October-2019/PTSD-is-More-Likely-in-Women-Than-Men.

Ward, Paul. *4 Rs of Trauma-Informed Ministry*. Seattle, WA: Direct Publishing, 2020. Kindle.

Washington, Kevin. "African American Cultural Competency Training Program." Online Training presented at the Boris Lawrence Henson Foundation, 2021. https://african-american-cultural-competency-training-.teachable.com/p/home-page.

Wave Trust. "Adverse Childhood Experiences." Digital Image. Wave Trust. Accessed December 14, 2023. https://www.wavetrust.org/adverse-childhood-experiences.

Weingreen, J. "The Case of the Daughters of Zelophchad." *Vetus Testamentum* 16, no. 4 (1966): 518–22. https://doi.org/10.2307/1516720.

Wendel, Alex R. "Trauma-Informed Theology or Theologically Informed Trauma?: Traumatic Experiences and Theological Method." *Journal of Reformed Theology* 16, no. 1–2 (2022): 3–26. DOI:10.1163/15697312-bja10022.

West, C.M. "Mammy, Sapphire, and Jezebel: Historical Images of Black Women and Their Implications for Psychotherapy." *Psychotherapy* 32, no. 3 (1995) 458–66, EBSCOhost.

Westenberg, Leonie. "When She Calls for Help'-Domestic Violence in Christian Families." *Social Sciences* 6, no. 3 (2017) 71, https://www-proquest-com.georgefox.idm.oclc.org/scholarly-journals/when-she-calls-help-domestic-violence-christian/docview/1952103788/se-2.

BIBLIOGRAPHY

Whaley, Arthur L. "Cultural Mistrust and Mental Health Services for African Americans: A Review and Meta-Analysis." *The Counseling Psychologist* 29, no. 4 (2001): 513–531. https://doi-org.georgefox.idm.oclc.org/10.1177/0011000001294003.

White House. "Fact Sheet: Reauthorization of the Violence Against Women Act (VAWA)." March 16, 2022. https://www.Whitehouse.gov/briefing-room/statements-releases/2022/03/16/fact-sheet-reauthorization-of-the-violence-against-women-act-vawa/.

White, Joseph L., and Thomas A. Parham. *The Psychology of Blacks, An African-American Perspective*. Englewood Cliffs, NJ: Prentice-Hall, 1990.

Whitfield, Charles L., et al. "Violent Childhood Experiences and the Risk of Intimate Partner Violence in Adults: Assessment in a Large Health Maintenance Organization." *Journal of Interpersonal Violence* 18, no. 2 (2003): 166–185.

Wiesel, Elie. *The Night Trilogy: Night, Dawn, Day*. New York: Hill & Wang, 2008.

Williams, Oliver J., and R. L. Becker. "Domestic Partner Abuse Treatment Programs and Cultural Competence: The Results of a National Survey." *Violence and Victims* 9, no. 3 (1994): 287–96, ProQuest.

Williams, Oliver, et al. "A Survey of Black Churches' Responses to Domestic Violence." *Social Work and Christianity* 46, no. 4 (Winter 2019): 21–38, ProQuest.

Wilson, Charles, et al. "Trauma-Informed Care." *Encyclopedia of Social Work* (November 4, 2013). https://doi.org/10.1093/acrefore/9780199975839.013.1063.

Wood, Hannelie J. "Gender Inequality: The Problem of Harmful, Patriarchal, Traditional and Cultural Gender Practices in the Church." *Hervormde Teologiese Studies* 75, no. 1 (2019). https://www.proquest.com/scholarly-journals/gender-inequality-problem-harmful-patriarchal/docview/2193085320/se-2.

Zamfir, Korinna. "Returning Women to Their Place? Religious Fundamentalism, Gender Bias and Violence Against Women." *Journal for the Study of Religions and Ideologies* 17, no. 51 (Winter 2018): 3. https://www.proquest.com/scholarly-journals/returning-women-their-place-religious/docview/2164138792/se-2.

Zippia. "Pastor Demographic and Statistics in the US" Zippia. Accessed September 26, 2023. https://www.zippia.com/pastor-jobs/demographics/.

www.ingramcontent.com/pod-product-compliance
Lightning Source LLC
Chambersburg PA
CBHW062041220426
43662CB00010B/1602